FABRIC
PHOTOS

Marjorie
Croner

 INTERWEAVE PRESS

The purchaser is hereby granted a license to use the patent-pending process described in this book for printing.

FABRIC PHOTOS
by
Marjorie Croner
Design by Signorella Graphics
llustrations by Ann Sabin
Photography by Joe Coca
Production by Marc M. Owens & Barbara Liebler

Library of Congress Catalog Number 89-24607
ISBN 0-934026-53-X

First printing: 15M:690:OB/CL
Second printing: 5M:591:OB

Third printing: 5M:292:OB
Fourth printing: 4M:493:OB

Library of Congress Cataloging-in-Publication Data
Croner, Marjorie
Fabric Photos / by Marjorie Croner
p.   cm.
ISBN 0-934026-53-X : $12.95
1. Textile Printing. 2. Photographs. I. Title.
TT852.C76 1989   89-24607
746.6'2—dc20 CIP

Interweave Press
201 East Fourth Street
Loveland, Colorado 80537

To my family and friends
for all the good memories we share

Acknowledgments

Photos by Stan Croner of our daughters and friends inspired quilts, bags, and other projects. Snapshots by Melanie Dimopoulous and Dan Wallace became eyegalsses cases, cosmetics bags, and my padded portrait. Ted Croner made proposal photos. Pat Mighell designed the medallion bracelet. Lisa Croner and Alice Wallace provided manuscript consultation, day or night. My mother and my Aunt Gwen supplied treasured pictures, enthusiasm, and good advice. Carolyn Holman photocopied skillfully. Forgotten snapshots of old friends, neighbors, and recital partners renewed glad memories of our wonderful hopeful days of youth and celebration. Editor Barbara Liebler gently fitted the pieces of this complex scrap quilt, added lovely parts, snipped dangling threads, and, with publisher Linda Ligon, shaped the book by hand. Thank you, all.

CONTENTS

Introduction 2
    Printing Your Photos—The Process In a Nutshell 12

Making the First Prints 13
    The Test 14
    The First Transfer—From Paper Copy to Printing Plate 16
    The Second Transfer—From Printing Plate to Fabric 17
    Printing Small Images on Shiny Fabrics 18
    Making a Bookmark 19
    Strip Printing Large Images or Coarse Fabrics 19
    The Printing Process 20

Other Ways to Print 23
    Wet Rubbing from Paper to Printing Plate 23
    Skimming 25
        Method 1 26
        Method 2 27
        Method 3 28

Introducing Color 29
    Test for Color Changes 30
        Coloring the Plate 30
        Coloring the Paper 31

Special Effects 33
    To Transfer Newsprint Ink 33
    To Transfer Other Printed Text 34
    To Print an Oval Image 34
    To Print an Odd-Shaped Image 34
    To Reverse an Image 35
    To Print a Figure with a Different Background 37
    To Make Border Prints from Snapshots 37
    To Accurately Place a Row of Images on Fabric 39
    To Print an Image Larger Than the Mending Fabric 40
    To Partially Block Out an Image 42
    To Print an Embossed Image 43
    To Make a Montage 43
    To Change a Facial Expression 43
    To Print a Mirror Image 44

Projects 45
   Soft Photo 46
   Book Cover 47
   Grandparents Pillow 50
      Slash-Fold-Topstitch 50
   Potholder 51
   Medallion Jewelry Box 54
   Wedding Invitation Box 58
   Graduation Flap Bag 61
   School Picture Doll 63
   Ribbon Print Drawstring Bag 66
   Folded Drawstring Bag with Trapunto 69
   Tap Dancers Pillow 72
   Easy-Does-It Crazy Quilt Pillow 76
   Modified Log Cabin Quilt 78
   Your Own Project 81
   Calculating Borders for a Block 82
   Chart for Drawstring Bags 83

Troubles and Fixes 85
   How to Fix an Imperfect Plate 85
   How to Deal with White Streaks on the Printing Plate 86
   How to Make a Darker Print 86
   How to Separate a Stuck Printing Plate from Fabric 86
   How to Straighten a Stretched Plate 86
   How to Remove Extra Adhesive from the Fabric Photo 87
   How to Make a Wider Border around your Photocopy Image 87
   How to Straighten and Control Shifty Fabrics 87
   How to Remove Transferability 87
   How to Soften a Release Print 87
   How to Flatten the Image if You Overstuffed It 87
   How to Register an Image 88

Afterword 89

Bibliography 90

Index 92

W hen I was a girl," my grandmother would say in a lilting voice. She'd tell me a tale, and then together we'd laugh at the joke she'd made. Because we both knew that she'd always been a grandmother. Her quilts brightened the farmhouse bedrooms. Her garden was a perfumed, pastel jungle of blossoms. When rainbows appeared above the fields of spiky corn where my dour grandfather labored, she taught me the names of the colors.

With her thin, lumpy back hunched above her sewing machine, her knees bouncing, her tiny feet rocking the treadle, she was a blend of grandmother and fairy godmother. Swoosh! from her magically graceful fingers emerged dolls, doll clothes, ruffled white eyelet dresses and pinafores for me; frothy pink housecoats and aprons for her daughter-in-law; embroidered tea towels and lace hankies for my other grand-

mother; and housedresses and aprons printed with tiny lavender flowers for herself. Her scrapbooks overflowed with pictures of bluebirds, bowers of roses, cupids, and romantic, dreaming girls. She owned a little brass bell from days when she'd been a teacher in a one-room school—"when I was a girl," she'd smile. She'd hug me and we would laugh.

And then, my dearest friend on earth was gone. "When I was a girl," she'd said, making it a game. But she had wanted me to know that she, too, had once been a girl.

When boxes of my grandmother's sewing supplies and photographs were delivered to me in Los Angeles, I was delighted. The boxes were a tangle of lace, thread, faded seam bindings, photographs, and mementos, all jumbled together. She looked grandmotherly, even in her wedding picture. I knew that my memories were dusting her face with age. I wished I'd asked her more questions. I wished I'd listened more carefully. I wished that in the girlhood photographs I could see the girl.

Over the years, as I searched the boxes for thread, crochet hooks, and blanket bindings, I separated the photo-

graphs and other mementos from the web of lace and rick-rack. But the old photographs looked sad and flat and lonely. So I put them back with the sewing supplies. That's where they seemed to want to be. When packages of my grandmother's Bondex® ("new, miracle discovery") surfaced, making me feel guilty about the mending that needed doing, it pleased me that my expert-seamstress grandmother had also used a convenient nonsewing aid. I used some for mending; later, I used the rest in a new way.

I cannot say that my grandmother's mending fabric guided me toward my printing discovery. In truth, her supplies nearly led me astray. Early mending fabrics had heavy, tapelike backings that clamped on fabric and hid the first images I tediously managed to transfer to their surface.

But I am ahead of the story.

In 1980, a quilt I'd made with my new sewing machine was accepted in an exhibit, a gladdening thing. I optimistically decided that my next would be made of fabric photographs. I had a collection of pictures made by pioneer photographers, and a few thousand old family photographs.

I didn't want to become a printer. I just wanted to put some pictures on fabric so I could give them new life. To learn how to do that, I enrolled in a workshop. What I learned was: there wasn't an easy method to print photographs on fabric.

I didn't believe it. It just didn't seem right to me that men could walk on the moon but I couldn't print photographs on fabric.

There was a process I had read about that used a special transfer paper in a color photocopy machine. If there had been a color Xerox machine in the northern California village we'd moved to, I would have tried it, but there wasn't. A good thing in the long run, but it didn't seem so then. I tried various time-consuming, frustrating, messy methods for transferring paper photocopies. Then I gave in, and worked with the methods I'd learned in the workshop. They were fascinating but expensive, time-consuming, messy techniques: blueprinting, brownprinting, Kwik-Printing®, gum printing, Inkodyeing®, photo-linening, silkscreen printing, and a few others, most of which require 1) when your full-sized negative has been made in your darkroom and 2) your sensitized cloth is freshly dry and ready for exposing, that 3) the sun be shining brightly.

To my surprise, I fell in love with this work, even with the second-hand enlarger I set up temporarily in the largest bathroom in the house, which my family gradually surrendered, having recognized it as my darkroom. I would wake joyfully in the middle of the night to turn the sensitizing fabric around to dry evenly, and spring from bed at 6 a.m. or earlier, eager for the day to begin.

While I enjoyed the process, I soon found that others were moved by the finished products. My mother was much in need of comfort after my father's long illness. She and her mother had been close. As a special gift, I made her a pillow. When she unwrapped the pillow, a portrait of her mother as a girl seated at the center of her family, she quietly rose from her chair, and holding the pillow close, carried it to her room. It was in the bed beside her the next morning.

Other people were comforted by the family photographs I was able to print for them. "My mother-in-law is more real to me on fabric than she was in life," one woman said. "We had our differences, but now I feel as if I understand her."

The fabric portraits amazed them and the process pleased me. I loved doing this. It seemed as if I had long, silent conversations with each person in each photograph. When I asked their owners questions about particular people, it turned out that I had often known what would occur later in their lives. It's there in the faces and stances of people. It's not a thing you can see with your eyes. It's a thing you feel with the part of you that makes things. When it's your own family, the understanding that you reach is deeply satisfying.

What I love most is the dramatic change in a photograph when it's put on fabric, stuffed and stitched: the people are round, warmed by a comforting nest of batting, soft and touchable again. The good feeling that's in the photograph flows out from it, into my eyes and hands as I work with it, and the glad feeling of celebration becomes part of me. That was true even with the brilliant blue color of blueprinted images, but later, after I'd developed my new process, it was startlingly true.

As a result of this work I loved, I soon

found myself in booths at craft fairs surrounded by silkscreened, blueprinted, and brownprinted bags, pillows, wall hangings, clothing, and other items that I'd made from the pioneer photographers' images and from a few of my family photographs. I exhibited my work in galleries, taught, and was offered commissions that I had to turn down because too many steps were in-

volved for copying each image.

Having to turn down a very large order for that reason in September of 1983 made me realize that I was as far from my goal as I'd been at the start. I still could not reach into my family albums and easily make fabric copies. It was frustrating that paper photocopiers were now producing sharp images in a moment, while it took me days to print a good image on fabric.

Asking local copier owners if I could load their machines with transfer paper provoked a discouraging response. "NO WAY!" the manager of the local general store shouted. "It would gunk up the machine." That had been the universal response to the idea from the ten other copier owners I'd already asked. Less vehement, but understandable. Copiers do get jammed easily. If I owned one, I wouldn't want to load it with anything but the machine's own paper, either.

But the manager of the general store had shocked himself by his outburst. He wanted to be helpful. "There's a lady in town prints photographs on fabric all kinds of ways," he said, in a kindly way. "Go round to the Art Center, she's got some real pretty bags and pillows and things showing over there. They'll tell you where she lives. Maybe she'll tell you how she does it." I didn't need to go to the Art Center. I knew where she lived. He meant me. I think that was the moment the idea arrived. I even think now that while he made paper copies of the photographs I'd brought with me, I walked to the sewing notions rack and took down a package of iron-on mending fabric, intending to use it for mending.

With fresh photocopies in my bicycle basket, I pedaled home and unlocked the door to my backyard studio, a former chicken coop. I went inside, and started cleaning up the chaos I'd left behind after making those earlier photoprint items. It was the chaos that gave me the idea. Two things that weren't supposed to be together got together. I stood there looking at them; it really did make sense. I decided to make a test. It took me quite a while, but it worked. Not perfectly, but well enough to make another test.

Many months and hundreds of tests later, a process more versatile than I'd imagined evolved. It was a primitive version of the process in this book. The process continues to grow swifter and easier. But even in its early stages, it allowed me to do too much. For weeks, I tested everything in sight—the mail, typewritten letters, the IRS instructions, grocery receipts. It was dizzying, like

running down a long hallway of doors that you are free to open, and unable to decide which one to try. When I decided

7

to go back to the door I'd originally opened, to print family photographs, my childhood wish that I could step through the barrier of a picture and walk around inside seemed suddenly to come true.

I had gotten the process working well on silk most of the time when all the photographs and other souvenirs of my grandmother's 1893 high school graduation seemed to fall together as a time capsule suitable for a quilt. The quilts I'd made and photoprint fabric objects I'd exhibited were machine sewn. If only I were as fine a hand-quilter as she'd been, I thought. I wondered if the handwritten words of her graduation essay, so beautifully penned so long ago, might be a substitute for stitches. Her hand had carefully made both words and stitches.

A Double Wedding Ring quilt, her specialty, was a design far beyond me, and a difficult format for photographs (I thought then). Her quilts had been made of cotton, but I thought she might enjoy the silk. When I began to print her picture on the silk charmeuse, I could imagine her delightedly saying, "Real silk! For me? Oh my!" I hoped the next step would work. The picture was larger than others I'd printed, and I hadn't yet developed a consistent technique. I struggled with that print and my fabric and iron until all at once I had it. Settled contentedly in the silk was the image of a sensitive young girl.

I picked up the fabric print to stretch and smooth it. Holding its edges, I moved my hands in opposite directions. When the silk threads shifted, the printed figure moved. She appeared to be walking. The hem of her dress went up and down, her shoulders rose and fell, her head tilted from side to side. The movement was comical, like that of a puppet, but I could see her as she must have been on the night of her graduation, an excited girl, scurrying up to the platform when her name was called.

She looked, surprisingly, as my oldest daughter had looked at her graduation, shy about the words she had to read, concerned about tripping in her long dress. And then I knew, the process of becoming the grandmother took time to develop, too. People are not born wise and sure of themselves, nor do they know from the beginning how to sew a quilt neatly. To learn to do anything takes time.

My colored pencils explored the details of her dress and features. Elora was there, hopefully peering into her future, dreaming as do all young girls of everlasting romantic love. Everlasting romantic love is not an easy thing to find, and so her lovely destiny was to comfort herself and others by creating with her hands warm, lovely fabric things. During the quiet coloring and peaceful sewing, I came to know her as she wished me to, as a young woman who seemed a friend.

She's in my everyday life now, softly touchable on fabric as she was before, a warm, comforting presence on the quilt that finally came to be. I used colors and a design that evolved from a blanket binding that Elora had saved, and I'd continued to save, for the right quilt to come along. Thread from one of her wooden spools helped me hand-quilt her portrait. A doily she had crocheted framed it.

Although I had wanted my first quilt using my new process to be a family tree, I decided instead that it would be Elora's, a memorial to her and her classmates. But the souvenirs of her high school graduation had other ideas.

There were only six graduates in the class, all women. The graduation ceremony took place in the windy, unsettled Great Plains in 1893, a time when people traveled by horse and buggy. My grandfather was then living several states away. They did not meet and marry until nine years later. So my first surprise was discovering that one of the six graduates had the same unpronounceable last name as my grandfather. It was written on the back of the graduate's photograph and listed in the program. My niece strongly resembles her. I accepted

that coincidence. It made sense that the classmate, probably my grandfather's cousin, introduced them nine years later and a few states away. Because I'd wanted it to be Elora Delia Johnson's own quilt, on her own before marriage, I was a bit disappointed that it suddenly had two of the four branches of my family tree. I was thinking it wasn't fair to my other two grandparents, particularly to my mother's father, an inventor. But near the end of the making of the quilt, while sewing the silk program, I looked down, and there—behold—was my inventor-grandfather's last name. It belonged to someone who sang that grad-

uation night as a member of the ladies' trio. My inventor-grandfather's family was also then living a few states away. So now the first quilt I was making by my new process was accidentally three branches of my family tree. I did not find the fourth branch printed in the program, but I suspect a representative was in the audience, that all the genetic pieces and threads that later accidentally wove me were probably there when Elora stepped up on the platform, and in a thin voice, trembling with stage fright at the sight of all the smiling faces, announced the title of her graduation recitation, "A Good Superstructure Presupposes a Good Substructure." It's a title that's as sweetly old-fashioned as the titles of our essays will be to people a hundred years from now. Elora had a fine, gentle sense of humor, and I think she wouldn't mind if the title makes you smile. One of the phrases that accidentally peeks out from behind the images on the quilt is surprisingly right and appropriate: "a good foundation to strengthen and support".

You will make similar discoveries when you print your family pictures. You can have fun while you sew, making up your own childhood-grownup entertainments. And, if you're a person who searches for the branches and off-branches of your family tree, you'll find many clues.

Looking for a theme to unify a family tree quilt, you may discover some themes unique to your family—that for generations people have been fascinated by and posed with wheeled vehicles, for example, or animals. There will be many surprises. That a noisy life-of-the-party

uncle always worriedly stands at the edge of a group portrait, or that a shy cousin appears at the middle of the group, even in the bride-and-groom-and-family-members lineup, blocking the bride.

Bigger surprises await you when you decide to do an autobiography quilt to introduce the person you are today to an

unknown person who will follow you in time. I discovered that a love of sewing and needlework went way back for me, and that I've always been the person who holds the baby—not just my brothers and sisters or my own children or nephews and nieces, but recently at a family reunion I must have gone to a neighbor's house to borrow a visiting one.

Because family photographs are made only when people are feeling happy—nobody ever goes running for the camera in the midst of an argument—you'll be seeing and working with the good moments of your life. It may help you, as it helped me, to clear up quite a few misconceptions.

It's not the whole reason for printing a fabric photograph, but I suspect that while you print, color, and sew small, lifelike memorials of the people and good moments of your life, you are going to be very enjoyably surprised. The real fabric of this craft is the fabric of your life.

PRINTING YOUR PHOTOS—THE PROCESS IN A NUTSHELL

A few minutes after warming up your iron, you can be sewing a fabric photograph you have printed. The supplies are simple: lightweight mending fabric, a photocopy of the photograph you want to print, and a piece of cloth to print it on. You'll need a household steam iron and the instructions on the following pages. You already have the skill. The decision to begin is the hardest part.

The process is simple:

First Transfer: from Paper to Printing Plate

Use an electric iron to press a piece of lightweight iron-on mending fabric onto a paper photocopy. Peel away the mending fabric. Its adhesive will pick up the image in reverse. The mending fabric is now a "printing plate".

Second Transfer: from Plate to Fabric

Iron the mending fabric printing plate onto your cloth. Peel away the mending fabric. The image will now be transferred to your cloth, facing the right way.

That's it. It's quick, easy, and inexpensive.

To get ready to print, first you need black-and-white photocopies. You can make them at your local library or copy shop or on any plain-paper, black-and-white photocopy machine.

The quality of your fabric print depends on the clarity of your photocopy.

pages of loose pictures in file folders in a flat box and set out for the copier.

When you press the copier's print button, you are selecting your fabric printing ink. Don't scrimp on the ink. Adjust the light-dark setting for the most important image on each page (don't use the copier's "automatic" or "photo" button). Try for a high-contrast

MAKING THE FIRST PRINTS

If the detail is crisp, the color a rich, dark black, and gray in the skin tones minimal, your fabric print will be all that you wish.

Small photos are easier to use than large ones for most fabric projects. They are also easier to print. To get the feel of the process, begin with small images and work up to large. Your driver's license photo is a good size to begin with, but take along several small photos when you plan your trip to the copier. Also take along a strip of dark paper about 3" by 3/4" to photocopy to use for a test. Any dark object or dark paper will do. To save time and expense, arrange groups of photos at home to fit on sheets of typing paper. Place these

Group your photos before going to the copy machine; tape to paper if you wish.

copy with black lines, white highlights, and gray tones only to show important contours. If the skin is all gray, it will darken on fabric and obliterate outlines of lips and eyes. If the copier is feeling unwell—copiers are moody—visit another copier.

Make several good copies of each page of photos. You'll need extras for tests and for patterns and coloring. Place the copies flat in a file folder. On the folder, write the copier's brand name, model number, location, and the date you made the copies. Now or on another trip later, try another copier. One may be better than another for this process.

On the way home, buy as many packages of white or light-colored iron-on mending fabric as you can afford. You'll find them in the sewing notions sections of fabric, grocery, and variety stores, near denim patches that are used for ironing onto torn blue jeans. You need the lighter-weight iron-on mending fabric, made for patching torn shirts or

13

bedsheets. It's packaged folded, about 6" or 7" wide, has one shiny side and one dull side, and you can mend with any you don't print with. (Although, for me, to use this magical printmaking cloth for anything so everyday and mundane seems utterly wasteful and bizarre.)

Buy a tube of iron cleaner for removing adhesive from your iron's soleplate during and after printing.

Buy fabric to print on if you haven't already found some likely-looking pieces in your bag of sewing scraps. The process will print on cloth of any fiber content, but I particularly like silk charmeuse for printing antique photographs. It takes images swiftly and clearly, and stretches slightly to produce softly rounded quilted figures. Consider how many pictures you can print on a half yard, and the cost of real silk may not seem so high. Heavyweight synthetic silks and satins also take transfers swiftly and are appropriate for old portraits.

Cottons and blends will transfer well if you follow the directions exactly and carefully. Batiste, lightweight muslin, and broadcloth are easier to print on, produce darker prints, and take the image more clearly than tightly woven fine cottons like sateens.

Secondhand stores are good places to find vintage fabrics, laces, and buttons to echo the spirit of those old family portraits if you don't have ancestral souvenirs of your own.

You also need a length of cotton fabric to fold into a flat, smooth pad. An old cotton sheet or pillowcase is ideal. If you don't have a piece of fabric like that at home, buy a piece of cotton or a used bed sheet while you're at the fabric store or the thrift shop. A yard of 44" fabric will do.

To set up for printing at home, just fold the cotton fabric or sheet four times to form a pad sixteen layers thick. Place this padding on a wood cutting board, Formica® counter, Masonite® clipboard, or any other hard, flat surface. Plug in your iron and set it at "wool". Get the fabric you wish to print, your scissors, a pencil, a wooden ruler, a watch with a second hand, and a few sheets each of cheap white typing paper for making paper peeling handles and erasable bond paper for ironing your print. There's your print studio, all set up!

Put your folded printing pad on a cutting board or countertop and gather your other equipment.

You can pull up a chair and do your printing sitting down.

THE TEST

Different copiers use different ink formulas and transfer technologies which affect at what temperature their images can be transferred most effectively. You'll need to run a simple test on a photocopy from any machine you haven't used before. The test will show you whether to peel your mending fabric off the photocopy while it's still hot, after it's cooled down a little, or after it has cooled completely.

Cut a piece of black photocopy image about 3/4" by 3" from the copy you made for the test, leaving a wide white paper margin at one end. Cut a piece of mending fabric 1/2" by 3¼".

Place a piece of typing paper on the folded pad to keep it clean. Put the dark photocopy strip, image side up, on the typing paper, and lay the mending fabric strip on top of it with the shiny, or glue, side down. Cut a 2" square of typing paper to use as a handle to peel the mending fabric off the image. Slip one edge of this handle 1/4" under the end of the mending fabric at the white margin.

On your printing pad, put typing paper, your black test strip face up, and your mending fabric strip shiny side down.

With the iron preheated to "wool", adhere the 1/4" margin of the mending fabric to the paper handle by touching the iron to it briefly. Then set the hot iron on top of the mending fabric, but not on the margin or the handle. Letting the iron's weight be the only pressure, slide it back and forth, side to side. Heat the pieces for 30 seconds. Don't apply pressure; just the weight of the iron is enough.

Remove the iron and stand it at a safe distance. Quickly, before the mending fabric and photocopy cool, hold the photocopy down on the hot padding by placing your fingertips or a wooden ruler on the photocopy's white paper margin and use the paper handle to peel back 1/3 of the hot mending tape from the hot photocopy.

Let it all cool for a minute or so. When the mending fabric is just warm, peel it back from the second 1/3 of the photocopy.

Move the pieces to a cooler surface. When completely cool, peel away the mending fabric from the final third of the photocopy.

Observe the results on the mending fabric (not the paper) onto which your photocopy image has been transferred. Compare the results to this drawing of three strips.

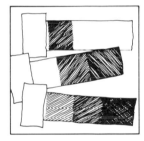

If your mending fabric strip looks like the upper drawing, then this copier's image transfers best **hot**. For all other photocopies from that machine, preheat your iron to "cotton" setting, preheat the padding for 10 seconds, place your copy and mending fabric on the padding and heat with the iron without pressure for 10 seconds, and peel the mending fabric off the photocopy immediately while both are still very hot. If your mending fabric strip looks like the center drawing, then all other prints from this copy machine should be peeled off when **warm**. Pre-

Your test strip may show that the image only appears if peeled hot, that it's best peeled warm, or that the darkest image shows when it's peeled cool.

15

heat your iron to "wool" setting, place the copy, mending fabric, and handle on the padding, and heat with no added pressure for about 20 seconds. Let the patch cool to warm, then peel up an edge to look at the image. If the image has appeared, peel the mending fabric off the photocopy.

If your mending fabric looks like the lower drawing, then prints from this copy machine are best peeled off when **cool**. For all other prints from that machine, use a "wool" setting and heat for 30 seconds. Let it cool completely before peeling.

Hot, *warm*, and *cool* peeling are three variations of the dry method for transferring the image to the printing plate. Once you've decided which variation works best for a particular copier, use it wherever the dry method appears throughout this book. Another method for this step, wet rubbing, will be introduced later.

THE FIRST TRANSFER—FROM PAPER COPY TO PRINTING PLATE

Now that you know how to get the best printing plate from a particular copy machine, transfer your driver's license picture or other small photo from the copy paper to the printing plate.

To do this, cut the photocopy out of the page, including a white paper margin as wide as possible along the narrowest, darkest edge, and white margins of any width along the other three edges. Place the mending fabric, shiny side down, on the photocopy on a hard surface. Use a lead pencil and ruler to trace the outline on the dull side of the mending fabric. Add a 1/4" margin along the edge that covers the wide paper margin. Cut the mending fabric the same size as the image along the other three edges. Prepare a paper handle by cutting a 2" strip from the edge of a piece of typing paper, scalloping the cut edge so you'll know which edge is absolutely straight.

Preheat your iron according to the instructions for hot, warm, or cool peeling. Place the photocopy, right side up, on the padding. If you are right-handed, turn the photocopy so the wide paper margin is at your left. Position the mending fabric shiny side down on the photocopy. Place the paper handle under the edge of the mending fabric, aligning the straight edge of the handle so that it just touches the dark edge of the

To transfer from the paper copy to the printing plate, use a "wool" or "cotton" setting and no pressure beyond the weight of the iron.

photocopy. With the hot iron, adhere the 1/4" margin of the mending fabric to the handle. Slide the iron lightly onto the surface of the plate to cover it completely. Avoid covering the handle. Remove your hand from the iron—it is important at this point to use no pressure but the weight of the iron. Slide the iron back and forth, side to side, so the steam vent holes are in different spots, and continue to heat for the amount of time

This fabric photo sits upright on a dresser.

tips to rub away the torn paper. Use the torn photocopy as a map to show you where those invisible-when-wet fibers are.

If you're not ready to print onto your fabric, store the mending fabric plate uncovered, image side up, on top of the peeled photocopy in a flat box. Write the date, printing technique, and other information on the back of the plate.

appropriate for your copy. Set the iron aside. Peel hot, warm, or cool as your test indicated, peeling back the mending fabric while holding the photocopy down on the padding.

If you are peeling while the plate is hot, do so quickly, being sure to pull in the direction of the threads (on grain), not diagonally. If you are peeling a warm or cool plate, peel slowly as you inspect the transferred image. If any details are not transferred, roll the mending fabric plate back into position, heat with the iron using slight pressure in the areas that have not transferred, and peel again. If the paper tears (or threatens to), loosen a dark corner or edge and peel from another direction toward the tear. If tearing continues, finish peeling the plate off and then dampen it and use your finger-

Hold the paper down as you peel back the mending fabric piece, pulling in the direction of the threads rather than diagonally.

THE SECOND TRANSFER—FROM PRINTING PLATE TO FABRIC

To transfer the image from the printing plate to your fabric, you'll need the iron, clean typing paper, padding, the fabric, and a wooden ruler. Check that your iron's soleplate is clean, and use cleaner if needed.

Before transferring the image on the printing plate to fabric, check to see that the paper handle is clean. If some of the black image came off onto the handle during the first transfer, replace it with a new one. To attach the new handle, place the plate, image side up, on a clean sheet of paper on the padding. Align the edge of the new paper strip with the edge of the image, and attach it with the tip of the heated iron.

The technique for transferring from plate to fabric depends on whether your fabric is a shiny synthetic or silk, or a rougher-textured natural fiber. The preparation steps are the same: cut or tear your fabric to size, adding a comfortably wide border on all sides. It's easy to cut away the excess later, but

17

impossible to make a small piece of fabric bigger if you misjudged. On the other hand, don't make your fabric so big it's hard to handle for this first print. If your fabric is stiff with sizing, swish it in suds, rinse, and iron it dry on the padding, stretching to remove all wrinkles. Then lift the fabric, put a piece of clean typing paper on the padding, and put the fabric, right side up, on the typing paper. Place the printing plate, shiny side down, on the fabric in the position you want it to print.

To prevent scorching, cover the fabric around the printing plate with clean typing paper or scrap fabric. If these get scorched, replace them.

Now the moment arrives when you can add pressure to your iron. In fact, pressure and heat are the most important elements in the final transfer, from plate to fabric.

PRINTING SMALL IMAGES ON SHINY FABRICS

Printing a small image on a shiny fabric is easier than printing a big image or printing on a rougher fabric. If your transferred plate is 3" by 5½" or smaller and your fabric is shiny (as for the bookmarks described below), you can print it by this simple method. With your dry iron preheated to "wool", iron the printing plate with pressure to firmly fasten it to the fabric. Cover the printing plate with a piece of typing paper. Increase the iron's temperature to "cotton". When it is fully heated, place the iron on the

Toe-to-knee was a common pose in my early years.

typing paper to fully cover the plate. Push down HARD on the iron for one full minute. Use both hands to press down. During this steady heating, change the iron's position a few times to change the placement of the steam vents, but don't lift it. Remove the typing paper after the full

For the final transfer, from printing plate to fabric, use a "cotton" setting and lots of pressure.

minute and quickly peel the printing plate away from the fabric while both are very hot. If the plate cools, or if it is stuck to any part of the fabric, reheat that section by ironing the plate with pressure, and then peel the hot plate away.

Your first print is now finished!

MAKING A BOOKMARK

A bookmark is an easy project for trying out your new photo printing technique. You'll need a length of wide satin ribbon, a photocopy that includes a figure small enough to fit on it, and a piece of mending fabric. For these book marks, I transferred the rectangular area that included the figure, colored the plate, and cut away the background before printing on the fabric.

Peeling at a hot, warm, or cool temperature as indicated by your test, transfer the photocopied image to the plate. When the plate cools, cut out the figure. Cut a length of satin ribbon a little longer than the finished length. Transfer the image to the ribbon with the "cotton" heat setting, pressure, and one minute of heat as described above. Peel immediately. You can use your fingernail to lift a corner of the printing plate and peel it quickly if the image is too odd a shape to add a peeling handle.

To prevent staining the book, lay the ribbon face down on typing paper and iron repeatedly on clean areas until the image no longer transfers to the paper. There will still be a strong image on the ribbon, so you needn't worry about losing it. Trim the ribbon's top and bottom to the finished length and unravel a bit to make a decorative fringe, or trim the ends with a bit of lace.

To print the other bookmark shown here, purchase a white cotton open-weave bookmark from the cross-stitch section of a craft store, and print it with the directions that follow for coarser weaves or natural fibers. Since the pur-

chased bookmark will already have a lace edging, there is no finishing needed.

My great-grandmother holds my mother.

STRIP PRINTING LARGE IMAGES OR COARSE FABRICS

Smooth, closely woven silks and synthetics accept prints easily, especially small images like those in the bookmark we just discussed. You can also print onto fabrics of coarser weave or other natural fibers, but the process is a little different. With these fabrics, the print must be forced into the cloth with heat and pressure. If you simply press the whole image with the flat iron, it will only print on the high points of the weave and miss the rest of the image. With this heat and pressure technique,

1. Place the photocopy on padding. On it put a piece of mending fabric shiny side down (with a paper handle attached), then cover with typing paper. Iron with no extra pressure.

2. Hold down the photocopy and grasp the paper handle with your other hand to peel the plate. Pull in the direction of the mending fabric threads, not diagonally.

3. When the plate cools, cut out the figure. Leave a tab for a paper handle, and attach it with an iron. Place it shiny side down on the satin ribbon and cover with typing paper.

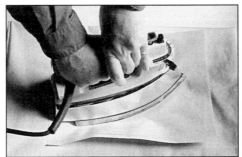

4. Using a "cotton" setting, iron with lots of pressure for a full minute.

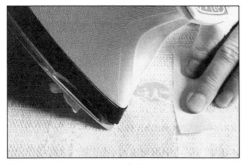

5. To print on coarse fabrics or natural fibers, rub the image into the fabric with the edge of the hot iron.

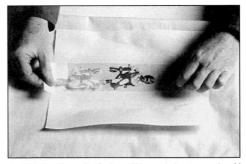

6. While the cloth is still very hot, peel off the printing plate. Again, pull in the direction of the fibers, not diagonally.

you can print cotton, linen, heavy canvas, felt, wool (including sweaters), terry cloth, belting, quilt batting, and even nylon mesh.

You can also print bigger images than the one discussed in the bookmark project using this technique. Mending fabric was designed to grab fibers. When given more heat and pressure than it was designed for, it shrinks and the edges release the image. If you attempt to print large images by simply putting a hot iron down on the printing plate and pushing hard as you did for the small print on satin ribbon, your fabric will have beautifully printed edges and a bubbly, unevenly-printed middle.

Using the edge of the hot iron as a scraping tool, force the image down into the fabric. Work one strip at a time, starting with the inch closest to the paper handle.

The best way to print larger images, coarser weaves, or natural fibers other than silk is to apply a great deal of pressure with the edge of your hot iron, working in strips about 1" wide. Make a printing plate from a somewhat larger image, perhaps 4" by 6". Cut away any unwanted image from the printing plate, leaving a tab or margin to attach a paper handle. Place the plate with its attached handle face down on a piece of coarser cotton fabric such as muslin. To prevent the fabric around the edges from scorching, cover it with typing paper.

Preheat your dry iron to "cotton".

Fasten the whole plate firmly to the cloth by sliding the iron lightly onto the plate beside the handle and then pressing more firmly as you slide it across the plate. This will keep the plate from shifting and smearing the image as you work.

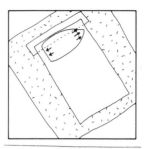

Hold the iron flat and slide it up and down the 1" strip, parallel to the paper handle.

To print the first strip, use the edge of the hot iron as a scraping tool, much as you would use a knife blade to spread hard butter. Tilt the iron and press the edge down hard onto the plate along the edge of the paper handle. Using enough pressure to force the image into the fibers, scrape the edge of the iron across the plate away from the handle for about 1". Then lower the lifted edge until the iron is flat. Still using pressure, hold the iron flat and slide it up and down this 1" strip, parallel to the handle. Then hold the iron steady and push down hard to heat the strip fully. Set the iron aside and peel the hot plate from the 1" strip of printed fabric.

Hang the printed strip over the edge of the padding or slip clean erasable bond paper between the print and the peeled portion of the plate. Print

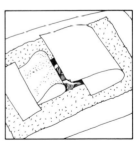

Transfer a strip, peel it, then protect that image with a piece of erasable bond paper before printing the next strip.

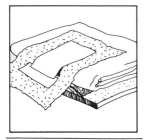

Instead of inserting paper to protect the printed strip, you can hang it over the edge of the padding away from the heat.

Make a bookmark of satin ribbon with the "Small Images on Shiny Fabrics" technique, or make one of cross-stitch fabric with the "Large Images or Coarse Fabrics" technique.

the adjoining 1" strip in the same way, including a narrow edge of the first printed strip.

Continue to heat, peel, and protect adjoining strips until you reach the last strip. Take time with that last strip. It's easy to say "Oh well, everything else looks good," and peel the plate too soon.

If the protective paper has stuck to the image, heat it and peel it away. There's your first strip print.

Use this strip printing process for images larger than about 4" and for printing onto coarse weaves; for small images on shiny synthetics or smooth silk, you can use the simpler method of 60 seconds of heat and pressure with a flat iron. For a small image on a coarse fabric, like the purchased bookmark discussed earlier, you may not need to work in 1" strips, but do use the edge of the iron to rub the image into the recesses of the cloth.

*T*here are other ways to make both the first transfer, from paper to printing plate, and the final transfer, from printing plate to fabric. The bookmark project used a dry method for the first transfer. This dry method works well with most black-and-white photocopies and with photocopies from some color copiers. It also will transfer words from inked typing ribbons, as well as colored and lead pencils, crayons,

OTHER WAYS TO PRINT

chalk, pastels, and acrylics, as you'll learn in the chapter on color. That's very useful if you want to transfer your drawings, tracings, or messages to fabric.

WET RUBBING FROM PAPER TO PRINTING PLATE

But what if you want to transfer a color picture directly from a magazine? Here's a wet rubbing method that will do the job. It will also make a darker print from a black-and-white photocopy than the dry method will.

Wet rubbing works especially well with colored magazine or brochure images (see the eyeglass case on page 45). The smoother the surface of the paper, the better. *Smithsonian* magazine images, for example, slide right off the slick paper. The process destroys the original printed image, and with some papers and inks, the image transfers easily onto the mending fabric plate but then washes off the plate if you don't work quickly. So try wet rubbing a small image from another page of the magazine before you attempt your real goal.

To transfer a paper image to the printing plate for a wet rubbing, prepare your materials as for the dry method. With your dry iron set on "wool", heat the mending patch on the image for a full minute rubbing the edge of the tilted iron against the plate. Allow it to cool completely while you assemble the following:

- Soap solution: 1 part dishwashing liquid, 4 parts comfortably warm (not hot) water in a shallow bowl
- Comfortably warm (not hot), clear rinse water in a wide bowl
- Old bath towel
- Cotton rag

Arrange the shallow bowl of soap solution, the wide bowl of rinse water, and the folded bath towel close to one another near a sink, with the cotton rag nearby. Temperature of the water is important; it should feel comfortably warm to the hands. If it's too hot for your hands, the heat-softened image will rub away. If uncomfortably cold, the paper fibers won't rub off. The bath towel is padding on which to hold the plate as you rub, and the cotton rag is a rubbing tool. Thumbs are the best tool for removing fibers; fingertips, palms, heels, and edges of hands are also excellent.

23

To soften and remove the top layer of paper, dip the cooled patch, paper side up, in the soap solution. Remove it before it is thoroughly wet. Tear away as much damp paper as comes away easily. Place the printing plate image side up on the folded towel and pick up the bits of torn paper with your fingernail. Roll away the remaining paper with your fingertips. The transferred image will be visible through a fuzzy, sudsy layer of paper fibers. The image is soft when warm and wet, so don't rub the plate against the bottom of the bowl or any other hard surface.

Gently peel away the wet paper from the printing plate, being careful not to scrape off any image with your fingernails.

Cup your hands under the plate in the clear water, and gently rub with your thumbs to remove all paper fibers from the plate.

To soften and remove the remaining paper fibers, immerse the printing plate, image side up, in the warm clear water. Cup your fingers under the plate and, holding it under water, gently roll the paper fibers off the surface with your thumbs. Begin at the edges while you learn how much pressure to apply, and move cautiously toward the most important part of the image. If paper remains on the surface,

soap again and work in clear water until all paper fragments are removed. Then place the plate on the towel, image side up, and skid the last tiny fibers off the surface with your fingers, or wrap the cotton rag around your finger and buff the fibers off the surface.

When it seems all paper fibers are gone, work again over the facial area of the image, especially the eyes. Invisible fibers are particularly fond of eyes. Rinse the plate in cold running water to remove all detergent and paper crumbs.

Place the plate, image side up, on the towel. Slide your hand across it to squeegee off standing water. Although the wet plate can be printed on fabric, a short drying time will reveal undetected paper fibers. Look closely while the plate is drying and after it is completely dry, and remove any paper fibers that you see. They will block part of the image when you transfer it to fabric. When you have a good, clean printing plate, transfer it to your fabric by the strip printing method, rubbing with the edge of your iron.

If the details of your wet-rubbed plate do not transfer to fabric, it's because they are blocked by paper fibers. Peel the printing plate from the fabric slowly, looking for this problem. If a section does not transfer, dampen the plate and place the plate and fabric on a hard smooth surface like a butcher block or countertop. Use pressure with the tip of the iron to transfer both the image and the paper fibers to the fabric. Peel the plate off the fabric print and then remove the dark paper fibers.

SKIMMING

Once the image is on your printing plate by dry peeling or wet rubbing, you can print it onto your fabric in either of two ways. The method that we've been using so far I call *releasing* because it transfers all of the image, any color that was added to the plate, and all of the adhesive that was on the mending fabric. This method works for photocopies and for all other images from other sources. This is the method used for the tests and the first prints, as well as the bookmark project. It produces the darkest possible print.

But the adhesive that release printing transfers along with the image causes a bit of stiffening of the printed cloth. You can soften the fabric print somewhat by stretching it on the bias to break the bond of the adhesive; the print will soften more as you work with it. Meanwhile the extra body makes sewing eas-

ier and helps photographed figures to hold their shape. This stiffening is less apparent on loose weaves and heavy fabrics.

Skimming is another technique for transferring an image from printing plate to fabric. Because it transfers no excess adhesive, the fabric remains flexible; the prints are soft to the eye and soft to the touch. Skimming produces one medium-dark print or multiple prints from one printing plate. The results are less predictable than release prints, though, and may require experimenting to find the right temperature for your iron and the right moment for peeling the plate.

The skimming technique will work with most plates from black-and-white photocopies. Plates made from colored magazines, or hand-colored areas of any plate, cannot be skimmed. (Colored images will be discussed more fully in the next chapter.)

The two faces of baby.

It's very easy to skim a layer of image from a plate's adhesive. It's also fun. You can print on fabrics or papers you wouldn't think were possible to print because the hot iron would melt them. If the plate was made from a really good photocopy, you might be able to print one dark gray fabric print and one very light gray fabric print; or two or more medium gray fabric prints (embroider or paint them or use them for special effects); or two or more prints on hand-made or other paper.

Then, when you've finished skim-ming, there might be enough image left on the plate to make a fabric print by the release method. To make a release fabric print from the plate's remaining image, soak the plate in water briefly before beginning the release transfer.

Here are three easy methods for skim-ming:

Skimming Method 1

Use this method for printing on deli-cate fabrics such as velvet and velveteen, ultrasuede, metallics and metallic bro-cades, and nylon (including nylon stock-ings for soft sculpture dolls, or even panty hose to wear!). Use it for fabrics that would melt under a hot iron, for pale images to embroider or paint, for projects that must remain soft such as scarves, or for printing on paper.

Transfer the photocopy to the print-ing plate by the dry method, if possible, though wet rubbing will also work. Heat the iron to its lowest temperature set-ting. Place the fabric you wish to print

The graduation portrait.

on the padding. Place the plate, image side down, on the fabric. Lightly iron the plate to adhere it to the fabric. Now, using the tip of the warm iron as if it were a pencil, rub only the black areas of the plate, beginning with the black area that is nearest the handle. Rub lightly if you want a pale trans-fer, or with pres-sure if you want a dark transfer. Tak-

Use Skimming Method 1 to print images on del-icate fabrics, including nylon stockings.

ing care not to change the plate's posi-tion, lift up a corner and peek at the fabric image. For a darker transfer, rub

This glasses case captures a moment of fun. Made from a color snapshot by Melanie Dimopoulos.

harder. If it's still not dark enough, increase the iron's temperature slightly and rub again, but take care not to rub the white areas of the plate. Transfer the image section by section until you've transferred the full image.

If your fabric print is dark, that indicates that there might be enough ink left on the plate to make another skimmed print. The image on the plate often still looks dark when all the ink that was available for skimming is used up, so judge by the fabric print rather than by the appearance of the printing plate.

Skimming Method 2

This is an easy method for a light print of a larger-than-iron-size image. Use it for projects that you plan to embroider, paint, or decorate in another way. I've tested Bondex® or Coats and Clark® mending fabric for the plate; if you use another brand, test a small image first. Some have adhesives that will suddenly transfer at the higher temperature this method requires.

Place the cloth you wish to print on the padding. With the iron temperature set at "wool", iron the cloth until it's hot. Place the printing plate face down on the hot cloth. Rub the back of the plate with a ruler, the heel of your hand, a brayer or any nearby cool object. Peek at the edge of the image. If it's not dark enough, slide your iron over the plate lightly and quickly. If any adhesive slides onto the cloth, briefly heat that section with the iron, let it cool, and then peel the plate.

For Skimming Method 2, heat the fabric, put the printing plate down on it, and rub with a ruler or other cool object.

Skimming Method 3

Use this method on sturdy fabric. You may have discovered it on your own when you made your first print.

Use Skimming Method 3 only on sturdy fabrics. Print the plate to fabric, let it cool, then rip the plate off the fabric.

If you follow the directions for "Printing Small Images on Shiny Fabrics", page 18, but let the plate cool down before you peel it away from the fabric, and if both you and the fabric are strong enough, you can tear the cool plate away from the fabric, taking most of

the adhesive away at the same time. The adhesive tends to retreat back into the mending fabric as it cools, leaving the cloth print soft and flexible.

There are many variables in the skimming process. Each print's darkness or lightness depends on the amount of ink on the plate, the pressure you apply with the iron, and the fabric. For dark prints that are washable, skim the image to synthetics.

Because there are so many variables, you need to experiment as you go. Test any new ingredient you add to the stew: fabric, new brand of mending fabric, copier, colored pencil or marker. When something unexpected happens, write down what you did at once; it's easy to remember a happy accident that produced an exciting result until the moment you try to recreate that result.

A bracelet for a special girl.

*I*f bright color is what you are after, you may want to try making fabric prints from a color copy machine. But be prepared for surprises when transferring color photocopies. A pink can become a green. Some color copies I've tried will show less color change if they are peeled while hot than if they are allowed to cool, but even then they lose some yellow.

I prefer to add color to a black-and-white image with colored pencils. Humans see colors more selectively and subjectively than color film and color copiers do. We focus on outlines and shapes. The office copier's black outline of a family photograph is more familiar and comforting than a color copier's bright hues. It's warm and loving and, when colored by hand, it's what I want in my family images. It's also more available, and unbelievably affordable—a few pennies per image.

Except for the piece using colored magazine images shown on page 45, the color in the pieces shown in this book comes from hand coloring a black-and-white image with pencils, either by coloring the plate or by coloring the finished fabric. For release prints that need to be washable, color the plate before printing the fabric. If the fabric won't need to be washed or dry cleaned, color directly on the printed fabric after the final transfer.

The easiest time to color is after the image is printed on fabric. There is no need to test your supplies. Did you color in a coloring book in grade school? That's all there is to it. Colored pencils are very easy to use. They don't spill or spread out onto fabric like paints and dyes. Just sharpen your colored pencils, and place the print on a hard surface. Stay inside the black lines and don't color skin tone over the shadows or the

INTRODUCING COLOR

tiny black eyes and lips. Color the lips terra cotta for a natural look. Make a tiny dot of white at the corner of an eye if you want it to look more open. When it looks better, STOP. That's the hard part of coloring—you want to continue.

Stay with one color family—all blues or greens—for peaceful harmony. Avoid bright colors, except in small amounts. To create the effect of an old photograph, use a variety of beiges, sands, and tiny accents of yellow for cheering things up.

You can rub some of the color off with a dry rag if you color too much, but you can't remove it all. The colors stain natural fibers if left on a long time. They will fade a bit if washed, but is anyone ever going to wash your velvet memory box? or a silk wall quilt? or even a pillow or doll?

A fabric print can also be colored directly with markers if it is a piece of cloth that will never need to be washed. If you color the finished print with a fabric dye that needs to be heat set, cover the printed image with typing paper and

29

use a hot iron to heat set the area. You can even place the printed fabric photo in a dyepot to color the entire fabric.

For objects that will need washing, color the printing plate instead. The adhesive will hold the color on the fabric permanently, and the item can then be machine washed with your regular laundry detergent. Use markers, or just dip the tips of your colored pencils in water to make them soft and use them like paints on the shiny surface of the plate. If you don't like the color, rinse off the plate and start over. You can color on top of the black on the plate. The color will print beneath the black.

If your photocopy is the cool-peeling type, you can color the paper photocopy before printing the plate. You don't even need to make a photocopy. Draw on any smooth-surfaced paper with colored or lead pencils, crayons, chalk, pastels, acrylics, water colors, some inks, or colored markers; typing that was made by an inked ribbon will work, too. Use the dry method to transfer your design to the mending fabric plate, letting it cool completely before peeling. Use the release method for the final transfer.

A bit of lace edging trims a medallion.

TEST FOR COLOR CHANGES

Some colored inks and pigments will change color when heated and transferred. You'll need to test your coloring supplies to discover how they transfer from coloring on the printing plate or from coloring the paper photocopy.

Coloring the Plate

Cut a long strip of mending fabric about 1" wide. With an iron preheated to "wool" setting, fasten a 1/4" margin of the mending fabric strip to the long edge of a piece of typing paper. Use a colored pencil or marker to write an identifying name or number on the paper. Beside the name, use the pencil or marker to draw a line that continues

To test for true color transfer from a hand-colored plate, draw with colored markers across both paper and mending fabric.

across the paper onto the shiny side of the mending fabric strip. If it's difficult to mark the mending fabric with the pencil, moisten the tip by dipping it into water. Keep a small, capped bottle of water nearby for this purpose.

Using the typing paper as a handle, transfer the colored strip of mending fabric to a piece of cloth by the release method. Look at the fabric print to see how each color transfers from plate to fabric.

Coloring the Paper

Use the same piece of paper to test for color changes that might occur when

To test for true color transfer from hand-colored paper, transfer colored lines from paper to mending fabric to cloth.

transfers are made from paper that has been hand colored. Cut another long strip of mending fabric. Position it to cross the colored lines. With your hot iron set at "wool", heat the mending fabric strip for 45 seconds without pressure. Let the paper cool and then peel the strip. Transfer the image from the plate to fabric by the release method. Look at this fabric print to see how each color transfers from paper to fabric.

Match the two transferred fabric pieces with the colored lines on the typing paper and pin them together for a record. Store this record with the coloring supplies you used.

Keep the paper and the two cloth test strips together as a permanent record.

A reticule for going dancing.

Images of my daughters' childhoods seem to tell a happy story.

Introducing Color

hile you may prefer to print all your photos exactly as they came out of your album, there are many other possibilities. Those photos can be the raw material for wild and crazy art, or they can be printed with different backgrounds so that Aunt Ethel and Uncle Albert show up better against the background, or people from several different photos can be brought together in one family grouping. Here are several ways to achieve some interesting special effects.

TO TRANSFER NEWSPRINT INK

What can you use newspaper images for? Everything. Consider the messages you can print using cut-up headline letters, the cartoon or advertising images, the pictures of your heroes that you can make into dolls and puppets, the cartoon or editorial that says it all across the front of your T-shirt.

All of those are for your private use. If you want to sell an item you make from those newspaper images, you'll need to get permission from the paper that printed them. Don't break the law. Shoplifting and image lifting are both illegal.

Here's a very easy method for transferring black ink from newspapers, telephone books, and other sources printed in black ink on newsprint paper. It's a dry method, so quick to do that it's astonishing.

Use the folded newspaper as its own padded base. You don't need the folded cotton padding. You also don't need a paper handle; just use one edge of the plate. Don't fasten that edge of the plate

SPECIAL EFFECTS

to the newspaper. If you'd like a paper handle, fasten it separately before placing the plate on the newspaper.

Turn your iron to its lowest setting. Place a piece of mending fabric on the image or text that you wish to transfer. Hold one edge of the mending fabric up from the paper. Slide the iron onto the section that's beside your hand. Slide the iron back and forth with some pressure for a few seconds. The ink will transfer almost immediately (even from newspapers a few years old). Heat as briefly as possible. Peel up the section you're ironing, periodically, while the plate's warm (if it cools, you'll fasten the fibers to the plate). If the image is not dark enough, lower the plate and iron a bit more with some pressure or increase the iron's temperature. Peel the mending fabric plate quickly as soon as the image has transferred.

Cut away any unwanted image from the plate, and transfer the image to your fabric with the release method. (Newsprint ink can't be skimmed.)

If you want to transfer colored newsprint ink, you'll need to use the wet rubbing method (page 23). The colored ink will be lighter than the original. So if you want to print the Sunday comics, you might prefer to peel the black ink, as instructed above, and color the plate with markers as described in "Coloring the Plate" on page 30. This dry peeling method is much quicker than wet rubbing, gives brighter colors, and you have the fun of coloring.

TO TRANSFER OTHER PRINTED TEXT

To transfer printed text from papers other than newsprint, such as the wedding invitation on the box shown on page 60, photocopy the text and transfer it to a plate by the dry method, peeling the plate away when it's either hot or cool. Plates peeled when they are warm do not skim well. Then skim the words to the fabric for a soft print with no excess adhesive.

To center the text, either skim it to a larger piece of fabric and then measure the printed area and cut the edges, or register the image as explained on pages 87 to 88.

TO PRINT AN OVAL IMAGE

If you have a rectangular image but want to print it as an oval, you have two choices. You can cut the plate to the shape, leaving a tab to attach a paper handle, or you can cut out a paper frame to the size and shape you want

One way to print an oval image is to cut the printing plate to an oval, leaving a tab for the paper handle.

and use a heated iron to fasten that stencil to the plate before transferring the image to fabric.

TO PRINT AN ODD-SHAPED IMAGE

To print an odd-shaped image such as the figures on the bookmarks on page 21, simply cut the plate precisely with no tab for a handle, iron to transfer it to the fabric, then use your fingernail to lift an edge and quickly peel it off the hot fabric.

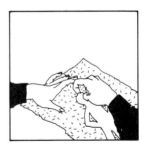

If your image is very irregular, print it with no handle and use your fingernail to lift and peel the hot plate.

TO REVERSE AN IMAGE

My grandfather at a stern moment.

In our part of the world we read from left to right. Because of this habit of moving our eyes to the right, a face looking to the right seems to be looking to the future while one looking to the left seems to be looking to the past. Of course not all of our photographs have people facing the way we want, so it is often helpful to be able to reverse an image. Here are four different methods.

You can *release an image to the back of a sheer fabric,* so that the image comes through to the front. I used this method for the woman printed in the medallion at the top of the Graduation Quilt (page 10). I wanted her to be facing her future, not backing into it. She is printed on sheer silk crepe de chine.

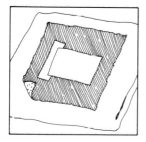

To reverse an image, release it to the back of a sheer fabric, then use the right side of the fabric for your project.

To reverse an image by this method, first transfer the image to a plate. With a warm iron on the padded board, fasten the plate to the wrong side of very sheer, thin fabric such as chiffon or organza. The image will print through the sheer cloth and appear on the right side, in reverse. Place the plate, shiny side up, on a hard, flat surface such as a kitchen countertop; place the sheer fabric, right side up, on top of it; and cover them with a clean piece of typing paper. Iron 1" strips of the cloth, but do NOT peel the cloth away from the plate. Do this cautiously but firmly, taking care not to smear the ink that transfers through the sheer fabric onto the paper. After ironing all the strips, when the image has fully transferred through the cloth, heat the full image with your iron and peel the cloth from the plate. Use the side of the cloth that was away from the printing plate as your print. It will be a reverse image.

Another way to reverse an image is to *transfer adhesive directly onto the print fabric, then iron an image onto it.* Cut a piece of mending fabric that is the size and shape of the image you wish to print. Using a "cotton" temperature setting and the padding, iron the mending fabric onto the fabric as if you were releasing a transferred plate. Peel off the hot mending fabric, leaving the adhesive on the fabric. Iron the photocopy onto the adhesive-covered fabric. Or achieve the same effect by fully releasing a print to fabric and then adding other images by ironing a photocopy directly onto the first image in the white spaces where there is adhesive.

Another way to reverse an image is to iron plain adhesive onto fabric, then transfer a photocopy image onto that area.

This technique works well with pencil drawings or with photocopies that are best peeled when they are cool. If you want to try this technique with a photocopy that works best when peeled hot, make a test first.

An example of this method of skimming can be seen on the Modern Old-Fashioned Crazy Quilt Pillow (page 75). The woman (my mother) emerging from the cream separator that the man (my grandfather) is cranking was cut out of a photocopy and ironed directly onto the released adhesive on the print.

You can also *iron directly onto the fabric.* Many, but not all, photocopy images can be transferred to fabric by direct ironing. These prints are usually lighter in value and less washable than prints made with a mending fabric transfer plate. Transfers to synthetic fabrics are darker than transfers to natural fibers. When a photocopy is so dark that the features are obliterated, sometimes direct ironing gives a better image than printing with a plate, as the lighter print lets the details show.

Using a "cotton" setting, iron the paper photocopy directly onto the cloth on the padded board. Because the photocopy process uses heat and pressure to adhere heat-sensitive ink to paper, the ink will also respond to heat and pressure so that it melts off the paper into the cloth. Iron with pressure on the photocopy, then flip it over and iron from the fabric side. Flip it back and peel up a corner of the photocopy to check the image. If it's not dark enough, place the photocopy and fabric on a hard, smooth surface such as a kitchen countertop and iron with pressure from either side. When the image has transferred, peel the paper off the fabric.

The fourth way to print a reverse image is to *transfer an image from one mending fabric plate to another.* This is a method that's fun to play with, though the result isn't predictable.

Transfer a small image to a mending fabric plate. Then treat it as if it were a paper photo-

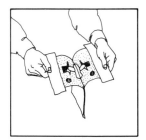

Or you can reverse an image by ironing a printing plate to another plate, then printing fabric from the second plate.

copy. When the plate is cool, cut a second plate the same size. Transfer the transfer to the second plate by heating the second plate for 45 seconds and peeling it warm from the transferred plate as if from a paper photocopy. You'll have two plates that are mirror images, both of which can be transferred to fabric. One will be darker than the other.

TO PRINT A FIGURE WITH A DIFFERENT BACKGROUND

Transfer the figure to a printing plate and the new background to another plate. Cut the figure out of its plate; do not add a peeling tab. Transfer this figure to the fabric but do not peel it. Place the background plate on top of the cutout plate and iron to transfer this background image, then peel both plates at the same time. If the figure doesn't peel off with the background just use your fingernail to lift an edge and peel it while it's still hot. The cutout figure will have acted as a mask to keep the background from printing over the figure. I used this technique to print figures in front of the telegram on the bag shown below.

To change background, cut out the figure, make a plate of the new background, then print figure and ground both at once.

TO MAKE BORDER PRINTS FROM SNAPSHOTS

Repeating a snapshot many times creates a rhythm that may be far more exciting than the original single image. That little snapshot, lost for decades in a box, has nothing about it that will make the world turn around, just a moment that was special to the posing people and to the person who snapped the picture. But when you repeat it on a bag, belt, or dress, the glad moment it represents suddenly becomes important.

Border prints from repeated snapshots cover this bag; the pocket shows small figures against a different background.

To print a *horizontal row of images with spaces between*, cut a separate piece of mending fabric for each image, including 1/4" margins at the top and bottom of each patch. Use one of these margins (either all the top margins or all the bottom margins) for your handle for the first transfer from paper to plate, saving the second margin for the second transfer. Transfer each image to its patch, taking care not to iron over the second margin of the plate. After the transfer, remove each peeling handle if

Hold the individual plates in place by attaching long strips of paper, iron to adhere the cloth, then turn over to print.

possible, and trim the vertical edges of each transferred plate to size.

Cut two paper strips that are long enough to join the entire series of plates in the row. Each of these long strips will be a paper handle that joins the images. On each long paper strip, mark the desired length of the row of images. Place the plates in a row, image side up, on a large piece of paper on the padded board. Cover the top margins of all the plates with one paper strip, the bottom margins of all the plates with the other paper strip. Adjust the placement of the images to fit evenly between your marks. With the tip of the heated iron, carefully fasten each long paper strip to each plate's top and bottom margins.

Moving this row of images may be difficult, so place the print cloth face down on top of the row of images and

A simple photo decorates this whole pillow cover.

use the iron to fasten it to each plate before turning the sandwich over for the full release transfer. Then print and peel each plate individually, beginning at either end of the row.

To print a *row of images that are joined* as if they were one long print, plan the joins where they're visually logical. A row of joined images will often fit the space you need to cover if you remove one edge of some or all of them. The plates may shrink slightly during the final transfer, so overlap to prevent broken spaces between them.

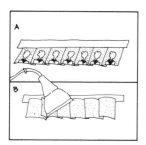

For a row of joined images, overlap the plates. Press hard with the iron on each upper layer to print at the join.

Prepare all the plates you'll need. Leave a 1/4" margin at both the top and the bottom of each plate but trim one vertical edge at precisely the spot where you want the image to end. Leave 1/4" extra image for overlap on the other vertical edge. Line up the plates on a large piece of paper, overlapping the unwanted edge of each plate with the adjoining plate's wanted edge. With a heated iron, fasten a long strip of paper along the entire top margin and another along the bottom. Move the strip to a cooler surface.

When making the transfer to fabric, the image from the overlap will transfer to the back of the adjoining plate. Pressure will be needed at the join to force the upper layer to print right up to the overlap. Use the tip of your hot iron to press along each join, forcing down the upper layer so it will print.

TO ACCURATELY PLACE A ROW OF IMAGES ON FABRIC

Measure the parallel distance from the raw edge of the print cloth to the nearest desired edge of the row of images, being sure to include any seam allowance. Using a ruler to make it perfectly straight, cut a strip of freezer paper to this measurement. Iron the shiny side of the freezer paper onto the cloth. Match the inner edge of the plates' long paper peeling handle with the inner edge of the freezer paper. Fasten the plates in position with the heated iron. Remove the freezer paper and make the final transfer to the cloth.

To line up a row of images, use a freezer paper mask to measure the correct distance in from the edge of the fabric.

You can use one of the plate's paper handles for placement, without using the freezer paper, if you cut it wide enough. After all the plates have been adhered to the wide paper strip, measure the correct distance from its inner edge and use a ruler to cut the outer edge. Pin this wide strip into position with its outer edge lined up with the outer edge of the cloth, and make the final transfer.

39

TO PRINT AN IMAGE LARGER
THAN THE MENDING FABRIC

You have an 8" by 10" wedding portrait, and you wish you had a piece of mending fabric that size. So do I. But until the mending fabric manufacturers decide to make bigger patches, we just have to improvise. With this technique, though, the big print is easy to make.

The first transfer, from paper to plate, is handled a little differently if you are peeling cool than if you are peeling hot.

If your photocopy is the type that is

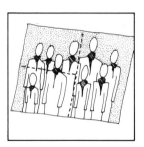

best peeled cool and your image is larger than the mending fabric, you'll need to make two or more printing plates. Plan the join in a white area or along a white vertical or horizontal line of the photocopy in an inconspicuous

Plan the joins to fall in an unimportant area of the image, preferably where there is a lot of white space.

area. If that's not possible, consider cutting away the photograph's edges to fit the size of the patch. The middle section is the important part of most family photographs, anyway. Never join two pieces on a small face, but for an enormous portrait, you can join on a white cheek if necessary.

The joins for the 8" by 10" photograph on the Graduation Flap Bag (page 62) were made horizontally along the lower part of the white gowns and vertically along the tassel of the hat of the girl at the left. If you look for it, you'll see it. If you don't know it's there, you won't notice. After a while you'll forget where you made the join. I joined many of the pieces for the large prints on the Log Cabin Quilt (back cover) so long ago that when I looked for the joins recently I hadn't a clue as to where they were. I do remember wishing for larger pieces of mending fabric. But I now wish I'd made that quilt of smaller copies of those pictures. I could sleep under a larger quilt made of smaller pictures but, much as I love those big trapunto stuffed pictures

My balancing act is displayed on my checkbook.

of my daughters, my home is not overly burdened with large expanses of empty walls to hang this wall quilt.

After you've decided where to place the join, just put two pieces of mending fabric side by side, face down on the photocopy, with their machine cut edges touching but not overlapping—if you overlap one piece with another, it's hard to print the join perfectly. Use one large piece of mending fabric for the larger, more important area of the image, and place the smaller pieces around it. Place a paper handle at their shared outer edge.

For the first transfer, fasten the mending fabric pieces to the image at the same time and heat them as if they were one piece. The pieces will shrink slightly and part from each other during the heating, but don't be concerned. Just continue to heat the whole image evenly all over with your iron. Cool the plate and peel it. The pieces will separate during peeling. When the plates have been peeled, cut their shared paper handle. Print the individual plates onto fabric as described below for large hot-peeling images.

If your photocopy is the type that is best peeled hot and your image is larger than the mending fabric, it's hard to keep the entire image hot enough to peel it. So it works better to cut the large paper photocopy into smaller pieces, including a white paper margin at an outer edge of each piece, and then treat each piece as a separate photocopy.

Cut each mending fabric piece 1/4" larger all around than its piece of photocopy. Place a photocopy piece on typing

A small group portrait.

paper or erasable bond paper on the padding. Position the mending fabric plate to overlap the three cut edges of the photocopy. Fasten a paper handle to the fourth edge on the white margin of the photocopy.

With the iron preheated to the "cotton" setting, preheat the padding for ten seconds. Place the typing paper, photocopy, mending fabric, and paper handle on the padding as you assembled them previously. After about ten seconds, slide the iron into position on the mending fabric and heat the plate for ten seconds. Transfer and peel the image from the photocopy. When hot, the mending fabric's overlapped edges will peel easily from the typing paper.

When all the plates have been made, cut the white margins from the three edges that have no handle. Now you have several plates that, when printed together, will make a complete image.

Special Effects

Many artists intentionally cut images apart. Their work gives others exciting new ways of viewing everyday life. You may wish to do that, too, by printing your large image with spaces between the pieces, or even juggling the pieces around and including other images. I can't do that with my family photographs. My reason for printing them is to put together again (symbolically, at least) the pieces that time parts.

First, transfer to fabric the largest, most important image and peel off the plate. Protect this printed fabric piece by covering it with erasable bond or typing paper before you transfer the adjoining print. It is then safe to iron on top of the protective paper when you make the adjoining fabric print. Never iron directly on a fabric photo.

Fit another transferred plate section in position. Don't overlap your first print; you can fill a gap with pencil when the print is finished, but you cannot remove the

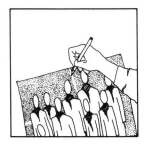

If there are white spaces on the printed cloth, use a soft lead pencil to darken areas as needed.

dark line that overlapping produces. Transfer this second plate and peel it off the fabric. Repeat for the other pieces.

Fill in any unprinted space between two sections with a lead pencil, making little dots on the fabric. Continue the shadow or the line that was broken, and the space won't show.

TO PARTIALLY BLOCK OUT AN IMAGE

Place the fabric on a hard, smooth surface such as a piece of Formica® or Masonite® or a butcher block, and put a piece of flat lace, mesh, or other openwork object on the fabric. Print a release image over the lace. Some of the image will print on the lace and the rest will print on the fabric, giving you an interesting pair of fabrics to work with.

For an interesting pair of fabrics, partially block an image with a piece of lace between the plate and the cloth.

TO PRINT AN EMBOSSED IMAGE

Once again, work on a hard, smooth surface such as a piece of Formica® or

To emboss an image, place an object below the cloth before skimming the plate to fabric against a hard, smooth surface.

Make a second print with the same plate for a pair of fabric photos with one embossed image dark and the other light.

Masonite® or a butcher block. Before the final transfer, place a leaf, piece of lace, or other object under the fabric where there will be a dark area of the image. Skim the plate to the fabric. The image will print darker where the fabric was raised by the leaf, lace, or other object. Then use the same plate to make a release print onto another piece of fabric. On this second print, the embossed area that is dark on the first print will be white, giving you another interesting pair of prints.

TO MAKE A MONTAGE

Since fabric photo prints are transparent, two images will seem to flow through one another if you overlap the images in printing. Print the first image onto fabric, place the printing plate for the second image, and then cover the whole surface with erasable bond paper before applying the iron to make the second print. You can then print a third image, also overlapping. Be sure to cover all image area with paper so that the hot iron never directly touches a printed image.

TO CHANGE A FACIAL EXPRESSION

To remove wrinkle lines or change the expression on a face, use the tip of a craft knife to scratch the line away from the copier paper before making the printing plate. After you transfer the image to the plate, use a soft pencil to draw a new smile, scowl, or lifted eyebrow. Or you can draw the new expression on the fabric after the final transfer. This is a wonderful way to make an interesting group of repeated images for a quilt.

Should I have changed the baby's expression?

43

TO PRINT A MIRROR IMAGE

Make two mirror-image prints by transferring from the printing plate to a folded piece of sheer fabric.

In a similar way, you can print two pictures in mirror image on one piece of sheer cloth such as chiffon or organza. It is easiest to do this with a wallet-size or smaller picture so the iron can easily cover the whole thing. First transfer the image to the mending fabric plate. Place the plate on the padding, image side up. Fold a piece of sheer fabric where you want the middle to be. With the heated iron, fasten the folded sheer cloth to the plate. Iron with pressure directly on the top layer of folded fabric until the image transfers through and appears clearly on the top layer. Peel apart. When you open the folded cloth you will find two images, side by side. One will be the reverse of the other. If you printed a face, you will now have an image of twins, looking either at each other or in opposite directions. You may be surprised to discover a feeling in their look—do these twins like each other or not?

An embroidery hoop makes a tidy finish for this photo of my father.

44

f you like to sew, or even if you don't, you'll probably think of a hundred ways to use fabric photos. Scattered through this book are pictures of projects I've made, offered as springboards for your own ideas. And on the next several pages are specific instructions for thirteen different ones that I've particularly enjoyed making.

You've noticed, I'm sure, that my taste and interests run toward the traditional, the nostalgic. I love the old photos, the old fabrics and laces, the hand-stitched, lovingly crafted look. The fact is, though, that my transfer technique can be applied in endless different ways. Sports hero patches appliquéd on a kid's jacket, high school yearbook photos on a back pack, wedding photos on a pillow case, seed packet art on a gardening apron, Andy Warhol-style collages on an artist's smock or boxer shorts—the only limits are your imagination and your ability to fit the original into a copy machine.

And keep in mind that you can photocopy not just photographs, but paintings, drawings, cartoons, actual objects like plants and flowers and children's

PROJECTS

handprints, newspaper headlines, concert programs, theater tickets, wine labels, and autographs. Don't forget that most copy machines can enlarge or reduce an image. Just think of the possibilities!

Use the wet rubbing technique to transfer images from colored magazines or brochures as Barbara Liebler did for this glasses case.

*F*or simplicity, let's start with a photograph in which all size and shape decisions have already been made. Here's Aunt Gwen, helpfully framed in a decorative cardboard mat. Choose a

SOFT PHOTO

similar photo of your own, photocopy it, and make a printing plate. Using

Make a print that includes the decorative mat. Color the image either before or after transferring it to cloth.

bleached muslin and the coarse fabric printing technique (page 19), make a

Layer the backing face down, the photo face up, and a piece of quilt batt. Sew through all layers at the top and both sides.

fabric photo print of the entire picture including the mat. Color it if you wish.

Place a sheet of lightweight quilt batting on the back of the fabric photo, and

Turn it right side out and hand stitch the bottom edge closed.

a piece of backing fabric face-to-face with the photo. Sew around both sides

To quilt the fabric photo, just sew along the inside edge of the mat by hand or machine.

and the top. Turn it right side out and hand stitch the bottom edge.

This photograph is like a quilting kit—the sewing lines are marked. To quilt it, just sew along the inside of the mat with hand or machine stitches.

*T*his simple cover can be made to fit a paperback book, pocket calendar, address book, or whatever. For the book cover shown here, I pleated the fabric to make pockets before print-

BOOK COVER

ing the photo onto it. You can make similar pockets or print on a flat piece of fabric.

To sew the cover, you'll need four pieces: the front printed fabric photo (I

You'll need four pieces: the front printed photo fabric, the back including the flap, a separate front flap, and a facing.

used white cotton fabric), a piece for the back that includes the back flap, a separate front flap, and a facing (I used a cotton calico fabric). The size of each will depend on the book you wish to cover. On the white cloth, print the fabric photo. Cut the front piece 1/2 inch larger on all four sides than the book's front cover. From the colored cloth, cut the front flap the same height as the front piece but 1/2 the width. To find the

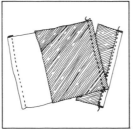

Hem 1/4" at the outer edge of each flap, and sew the left edge of the fabric photo to the back book cover.

width of the back piece that includes the back flap, add the width of the front piece plus the width of the front flap plus the thickness of the book; use the height of the front as the height of the back. Cut a piece of colored cloth to these dimensions for the back. Save the scraps to cut the facing later.

Right sides facing, sew the right edge of the fabric photo to the front flap. Sew the left edge of the photo to the back piece. At the outer edge of each flap, fold in and sew a 1/4" hem. Fold the flaps back, right sides together, and pin.

If you wish to pad the cover with quilt batting, cut it the same size as the folded cover, pin it to the back of the cover, and include it when you sew the book cover together.

Now cut the facing the same height as the front cover and wide enough to overlap each flap by an inch. Lay this on

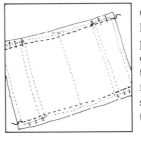

Cut a facing and lay it on the pinned book cover to overlap the folded-back flaps. Sew 1/2" seams along the top and bottom.

the pinned bookcover to overlap the folded-back flaps.

Sew 1/2 seams along the top and bottom to join flaps, cover, and facing (and batting if you are using it). You need only two seams. Clip the corners.

Turn the cover right side out and insert the front and back covers of your book under the flaps.

A soft photo is an easy
project—the decorative mat
is printed along with the
photo, and quilting along
the edge adds a finishing
touch.
Instructions are on page 46.

This simple book cover can
be made to fit a paperback
book, pocket calendar,
address book, or
sketchbook. I pleated the
cover to make pockets, but
you can also make it with a
flat cover.
Instructions are on page 47.

*T*his soft photo of my great grandparents is simply a black-and-white print on a colored fabric—an easy way to add color. Elaine Lackey designed and made it. With a loop sewn to

GRANDPARENTS PILLOW

the back, it can hang on a wall.

Use skimming method 1 or 3 (page 26 or 28) to transfer a photocopy image to a colored fabric. Quilt it if you wish.

Mark the opening on the wrong side of the pillow top, machine stitch to reinforce the line, and cut 1/4" inside it.

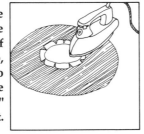

Then set the fabric photo into the pillow top by the **slash-fold-topstitch** method. Mark the opening on the wrong side of the pillow top fabric, and machine sew along your mark to reinforce the fabric. Mark a cutting line 1/4" inside the reinforcing stitching. Cut on this

Clip to the stitching and fold back the tabs to the wrong side, taking care to make a smooth line. Iron in place.

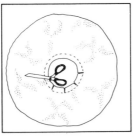

line and slash to the stitching as often as needed to let the fabric fold back smoothly. Fold the slashed edge back

smoothly to the machine-stitched line and iron it to the wrong side of the opening. Position this cutout on top of the quilted photoprint and pin it in place. Topstitch close to the fold with matching

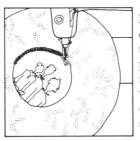

Position the cutout on top of the quilted photoprint, pin it, and topstitch with machine embroidery or a straight stitch.

thread or machine embroidery, catching in a lace edging if you wish.

Draw a circle on the back of the fabric for the outside edge of the pillow, then

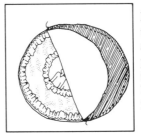

Pin lace edging to the pillow top and stitch in place, then sew the top to the backing with a 1/2" seam.

cut 1/2" outside this line. Pin lace edging to the front piece, right sides together, matching the outer edges, and sew it in place.

Cut the fabric for the back of the pillow the same size and shape as the front. Pin the back to the front, right sides together, and sew 1/2" from the edge all around except for a 3" opening. Trim and clip the seam allowance, then turn the pillow cover right side out. Stuff it and close the opening with invisible hand stitches.

My artist friend Elaine Lackey calls the two pieces she made from small snapshots of her daughter-in-law, who's expecting a baby, "potholders". I call them works of

POTHOLDER

art, and wish she hadn't sewn on the potholder loops. She's planning a baby quilt from those images. It's her way of working out a design. It's my way, too— my daughters call me the potholder queen. If you tell yourself you're making a potholder, you're free to take some risks, and whatever happens, the object you make will have some use.

When designing your photoprint block, you can either start with a projected finished size and add borders to the photo to make it that size, as in the Tap Dancers Trapunto Pillow, page 72, or work your way out from the edge of the photograph, sewing on borders until the object seems to decide its own size and shape. This blue potholder, which became a nine-patch quilt block, simply grew by the second method.

Make several prints of the same photograph, and choose the best five prints. Cut them into squares. Choose a com-

Make five prints of your photo and cut four squares of another fabric. Sew them together in the nine-block pattern.

plementary fabric and cut four more squares of the same size as the photo prints. Sew them together in the nine-block pattern.

Choose other complementary fabrics for borders. For the blue potholder, Elaine used piping for the first border. Keep adding borders, either all the same width or progressively wider, until you are happy with the finished look.

Place a sheet of quilt batting on the back of the finished photoprint fabric, and a backing fabric face-to-face with the front. For the loop, make a narrow band of the same fabric as the outer border, turning in the raw edges and machine stitching close to the edge. Fold this into a loop and put it between the front and back fabrics at an upper corner, with the raw ends of the loop stick-

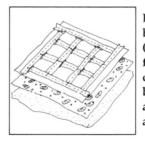

Layer the backing fabric (face up), loop, front fabric (face down), and batting. Sew along both sides and the top.

ing out the corner. Sew around three sides, catching the ends of the loop as you sew that corner. Turn the potholder right side out and hand stitch the other side.

To quilt it, sew in the valley where the squares join. If your thread matches and you sew carefully, this line of stitching will be nearly invisible.

**Printing your photo on
colored fabric adds life to a
portrait. Set the photo into
the pillow top with an easy
method; see the
instructions on page 50.**

Work out your design ideas
on a small scale by making
potholders. My brown one
is an experiment in
overlapping images; the
blue one is described on
page 51.

*T*his is a lovely but easy gift. It's a fine way to share a treasured photograph or to introduce a great-grandmother to a child.

The lid of the box can display photo

MEDALLION JEWELRY BOX

medallions of various sizes. You can use heavy fabrics, such as this dark green velvet, or lighter weights in a solid color or a flowered print. If you'd like to make a soft box, just cut each piece of mat board slightly smaller and wrap it with a piece of quilt batting before covering it. Make the box larger or smaller to fit your images or to serve your needs. To hold the wedding band my father gave my mother, I made a miniature box of tiny snapshots from their first married year.

Cut cardboard oval for the medallion. Cut the fabric photo 1/2" bigger all around, and sew a basting thread near the edge.

To make the medallion, first print and color the image. Then cut a cardboard oval to the size and shape of the finished medallion. Cut the fabric photo 1/2" larger on all sides than its finished oval shape, and hand sew a basting line around it just outside the finished size. Place a piece of batting between the photo and the cardboard, and pull the basting thread tight to pull the seam

allowance around the back of the cardboard. Knot the basting thread so that it stays tight, and iron the raw edge lightly to flatten it. If you prefer, you can transfer an oval image as described on page 34.

To make the box, you'll need a craft knife, a metal ruler or straightedge for cutting, cardboard from a tablet for a right-angle template, a ruler, a pencil, scrap cardboard to protect the tabletop from cuts, and some fabric glue.

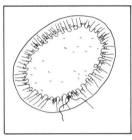

Pull the basting thread to tighten the photoprint around the cardboard and batting, and knot it. Iron the back flat.

You'll need the fabric photo medallion, a lace doily, 1/4 yard of green velvet fabric, a small piece of lining fabric for the inside bottom of the box, some cardboard to make the sides stiff, and some batting. Cut the green velvet into these pieces:

1 piece 7⅛" by 13" for the lid and lining

1 piece 7⅛" by 7⅛" for the base of the box

Center the doily and medallion on the velvet lid fabric, and hand stitch them in place.

1 piece 25" by 6" for the sides

Cut one piece of lining fabric 7" by 7". Cut one 6" by 6" piece of batting to pad the base lining. Cut mat board or other cardboard as follows:

2 pieces 6⅛" by 6⅛" for lid and base

4 pieces 2½" by 6" for sides

1 piece 6" by 6" for lining the base

After you have gathered all the pieces, make the lid of the box. Right

Slip the cardboard lid into the pocket, fold in the raw edges, and hand stitch the opening closed.

sides facing, match the two short ends of the 13" velvet piece. Sew the two sides with a 1/2" seam. Clip the corners and turn it right side out. Center the doily and medallion on one sewn piece, placing the folded edge below the picture. By hand, sew the picture and doily to the top thickness of velvet. Insert a 6⅛" piece of mat board into the velvet pocket. Fold the raw edges to the inside and slipstitch the opening closed.

To make the sides, fold the long green velvet strip right sides facing, matching

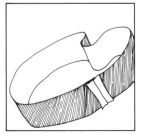

To make the sides, fold the long strip right sides together, matching the short ends, and sew a 1/2" seam. Press it open.

the two short ends. Sew a 1/2" seam across the short end. Press that seam open. Fold the long joined strip in half

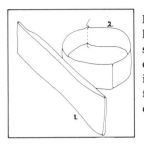

Fold the strip lengthwise and sew in the valley of the seam. Fold it at that seam to find the opposite corner of the box.

lengthwise, wrong sides together, matching the long raw edges. This piece will become pockets for the mat board sides; the fold will be the top edge, the raw edges the bottom. To form the first corner, sew in the valley of the seam starting at the fold and stopping 1/2" in from the raw edge. Fold the strip at the

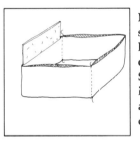

Match the two seams to find the locations for the other two seams. Slip cardboard in the pockets and sew them closed.

seam to find the middle; this will be the opposite corner of the box, 12" from the seam. Mark the spot and topstitch starting at the fold and ending 1/2" from the raw edges. Fold the strip again, matching the two sewn corners to find locations for the other two corners. Mark, pin, and sew them. Insert the four mat board sides of the box into the four pockets. Turn in and pin the bottom raw edges, and sew them either by hand or by machine with a zipper foot.

To make the base, center the 6⅛" mat board square on the wrong side of the 7" velvet square. Fold the margins inside

Glue batting to the cardboard base lining, cover with lining fabric, and glue the lining piece to the base piece.

and glue them to the mat board. Hand sew the base of the box to the sides.

To make the base lining, glue batting to the remaining piece of cardboard. Batting side down, center the cardboard on the wrong side of the lining fabric. Pull the edges of the lining fabric around the cardboard and glue them down. Insert this lined base into the bottom of the box.

Hand stitch the pieces together.

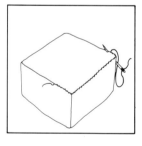

To attach the lid, slipstitch the back edge of the lid to the upper edge of the back of the box.

A photoprint medallion
decorates this jewelry
box—it could also decorate
other projects or become a
pendant or pin by itself.
Instructions for the
Medallion Jewelry Box
begin on page 54.

Projects

he wedding invitation text was skimmed to velvet for this special box made to commemorate my grand-parents' wedding. It would be a good idea to practice skimming onto a scrap

WEDDING INVITATION BOX

of velvet before attempting the final print.

To print the velvet for the lid of the box, use the dry method, peeled either hot or cool, to transfer the words to the printing plate. Plates peeled when warm do not skim very well. Attach a paper handle at the top of the text.

Lay the velvet on the padding with the pile slanting to the right. Smooth it by ironing in the direction of the pile.

To transfer an image onto velvet, the pile must lie flat and the iron must move only in the direction of the flattened pile. Cut a piece of velvet larger than you will need for the top of the box. Lay this piece of velvet on the padding so that the pile slants to your right. To smooth the pile

Skim the words from the printing plate to the velvet, rubbing only the black areas with the tip of the warm iron.

in the direction it already lies, pull a warm iron across the fabric from left to right. Put the printing plate face down on the velvet with the paper handle on the left, centering by eye. Skim the image from the plate to the velvet. Be sure that you move your iron only in the direction of the flattened pile (left to right),

On the cardboard lid, glue a 3" square of batting and then a 6" square on top of that. This makes a dome-shaped lid.

and that you only rub the text with the tip of your iron—do not rub the white areas.

To make the lid of the box, cut a 6¼" square of mat board for the rigid inside of the lid and glue a 3" square of quilt

Fold the lid lining fabric in half, then center it on the text. When centered, unfold it and cut the top to match.

batting to the center. Then place a 6" square of quilt batting on top of the 3" square and glue it to the edges of the mat board. This makes the padding slightly dome-shaped. To cover this rigid center, cut a 7¼" square of velvet for the lid lining. Fold the lid lining piece at the center and place it on the printed velvet text, using the fold line as the center line. Adjust the placement until the lining is centered on the text both side to side and top to bottom. When it is centered, unfold the lining and use it as a pattern to cut the text piece the same size. Right sides facing, sew the lid lining and printed text pieces together along the two sides and below the text with 1/2" seams. Turn right sides out and insert the padded mat board so that the batting

Slip the padded cardboard for the lid into the fabric pocket, with the batting below the text, and sew the back edge closed.

is beneath the text. Tuck in the raw edges and slipstitch the opening closed.

To complete the box, make each side separately. Make four cardboard side pieces, each 6" square with a cutout oval for a fabric photo. Use the slash-fold-insert method shown on page 50 to cover each side piece with a 7" square of velvet, gluing the tabs to the back of the card-

Make the cardboard sides with oval cutouts and cover them with fabric. Glue the quilted fabric photos in the openings.

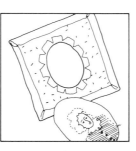

board rather than sewing them. Print, color, and quilt four fabric photos and glue them in position behind each open-

ing. Cut four pieces of cardboard, each 5⅞" square, and cover each with lining fabric (either more velvet or a lighter fabric) for the inside of the box. Glue each of these four lining pieces to each of the four framed photo side pieces of the box.

Cut two cardboard squares for the bottom of the box, 6⅛" square for the outside and 5⅞" square for the inside. Cover the outer piece with velvet, gluing the edges to the cardboard. Cover the inner piece with batting and a fabric print so there will be a surprise picture on the inside bottom of the box. Glue the outer and inner bottom pieces together, centering the inner piece.

Glue a lining-covered cardboard square to the back of each side piece. This protects the backs of the fabric photos.

Assemble the box by hand sewing the six panels together and then sewing decorative cord along each edge.

Line the bottom with a padded photoprint over a square of cardboard. Assemble the box by hand, then add trim.

59

Commemorate a special occasion with a momento box like this one celebrating my grandparents' wedding. There's even a surprise fabric photo on the inside bottom of the box. Instructions begin on page 58.

A large photo transfer makes a good decoration for the flap of a bag. Print the large photo as described on page 40, "To Print an Image Larger Than the Mending Fabric". For

GRADUATION FLAP BAG

this graduation photo of my daughter and two friends, I used a vertical join along the white tassel of the girl on the left and a horizontal join about an inch up from the bottom where the photo is mostly white and where a white finger provides a bit of horizontal line.

Put the completed, colored fabric print on a piece of quilt batting and quilt as desired—I simply outlined each girl

Sew the top edge of the flap to the narrow edge of the bag fabric, right sides together. Fold and sew the bag sides.

and outlined the entire photo. Square the fabric photo after you have quilted it.

To make the flap for a simple lined bag, sew this quilted print, right sides facing, to a lining fabric along the sides and bottom of the fabric photo. Clip the corners, and turn the flap right side out. Cut a piece of fabric for the bag measuring 3" wider than the flap and twice its height plus 5". Cut a piece of lining fabric

exactly the same size as the bag fabric. Join the flap to the bag by sewing the right side of the flap at its top, raw edge to the right side of the narrow end of the bag's back piece. Fold the bag fabric in half, right sides together, so that its raw edges meet; sew 1/2" seams on the sides. Fold the lining fabric in half, right sides together, and sew the sides with 1/2" seams, stopping 1/2" from the raw edge. Turn the bag right side out and slip it

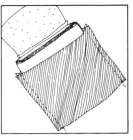

Slip the bag, right side out, into the lining, wrong side out, and sew the top front edge.

into the pocket of the lining, which is still wrong side out. Machine stitch the top front edge with a 1/2" seam. Turn the lining into the bag and hand sew the top of the lining to the base of the flap on the inside.

A photoprint pocket sewn to the lining can be a nice surprise inside the bag. Sew the pocket to the lining piece before assembling the bag.

Turn the lining into the bag and hand sew the top back of the lining to the base of the flap on the inside.

A large photo makes a dramatic statement on the flap of a bag. Read how to make it on page 61.

𝒰se these instructions for making stuffed dolls of any size. The dolls shown here will fit a dollhouse that's scaled 1" to a foot.

You can use a school portrait or snap-

SCHOOL PICTURE DOLL

shot; take a snapshot if you need to. You'll need one good photocopy and one scrap photocopy of the same picture for a pattern. For this scrap copy, you can use any copy made when you tested the copier's darkness setting. You will also need a black or mottled-black photocopy for printing the back of the head and the Mary Jane shoes. You'll need fabric for the doll—any skin-colored cotton-polyester blend or 100% cotton. Also get thread that matches the fabric, Fray-Check®, polyester stuffing, and fabric glue. You'll need colored pencils for lips and hair highlights. Berol Prismacolor® terra cotta is good for lips. Buy mending fabric and freezer paper if you don't have enough at home. You'll also need scraps of fabric and trim for the doll clothes.

Skim the poor photocopy to the dull side of the freezer paper by ironing it directly with no mending fabric printing plate.

To cut out the doll's body, first make a pattern from freezer paper with this easy method: place a piece of freezer paper, shiny side down, on the padding. Put the poor photocopy, face down, on the dull side of the freezer paper. With the iron at "cotton" setting, iron the photocopy lightly to skim the image to the freezer paper. This printed face on paper is the beginning of a pattern for cutting out the doll's body. Discard the scrap photocopy.

Use a ruler to draw a line that bisects the paper-printed face and extends down longer than the desired height of the doll's body. (My dolls, made from 1¼" by 2¼" pictures, are about 5¼" tall when stuffed.) Draw the outline of the body. Draw curves, not sharp corners. If the child has long hair, shorten it above the shoulders so you'll have the neckline to sew.

63

Draw the outstretched arms to equal the total height of the doll. Fold the pattern in half along the line to make the two sides even and cut it out.

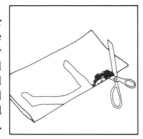

Draw a center line below the face, then draw the body around that center. Fold the paper and cut on the pencil line.

Transfer the good photocopy to mending fabric. For a washable doll, color the lips and hair on this printing plate. If you prefer, you can color the fabric photo later. Cut away the clothes from the plate by cutting on the collar line (or the chin line if the neck is dark

Make a plate from the good photocopy, color it, and cut away below the collar or chin. Transfer it to flesh-colored fabric.

or if the neck angles to the side). Don't cut away the background above and around the head; printing it on fabric will prevent fraying. Position the cut plate on the flesh-colored fabric with enough room below for cutting out the body, and transfer it to the fabric by the release method.

Turn the photo-printed fabric wrong side up on the padding. Protect the padding from the doll's printed face with clean typing paper. Carefully place the

freezer paper pattern shiny side down on the back of the fabric, lining up the face exactly. With heated iron, fasten the freezer-paper pattern in position on the wrong side of the doll fabric. Iron on the freezer paper's dull side (the side you drew on), not the shiny side. This gives you an easy pattern to follow and stabilizes the fabric as you sew the tight curves.

Pin this fabric for the doll front to another piece of flesh-colored fabric for the doll back, right sides facing. Sew the

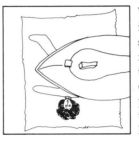

With a warm iron, fasten the shiny side of the freezer paper to the wrong side of the fabric photo, matching the printed heads.

two pieces together at the edge of the paper pattern with a short machine stitch, leaving a long opening in the side of the torso for turning and stuffing. Run a line of FrayCheck® just outside the seamline. When it's dry, trim the fabric about 1/8" outside the sewn line and clip the curves. Pull off the freezer paper pattern. Using tweezers, turn the doll right side out.

Right sides together, sew the front to the back along the paper pattern, leaving an opening. Peel off the freezer paper.

To print the back of the head, first stuff the head lightly with polyester stuffing. With the mottled-black photocopy, make a printing plate large enough for the back of the head plus the shoes. Cut it to the desired shape for the lower part of the hair, slightly larger than the sewn edges of the head. Place the partly stuffed head face down on clean typing paper on the padding. Position the plate. With your iron at its lowest setting, transfer the black areas by gently stroking the iron's tip along the plate. You can

Transfer a thin line of black from the plate to the tip of each foot to make the shoes.

Transfer black ink from the printing plate to the back of the head by stroking with the tip of the hot iron.

"draw" onto the seamline by holding the doll, or you can fill in the edges with a very soft black pencil.

To print the shoes, cut strips of the transferred black plate to shape and iron them as you did for the head. Or you can "paint" the black on by holding a larger plate in position and stroking the sewn sole line with your iron. Make the shoes very narrow to prevent a clodhopper, bumpy look. You can print the shoes after you make the doll's clothes if you prefer.

Stuff the rest of the head and the doll's body and sew up the torso side.

Clothes can be as elaborate as you wish. Revive that technique you learned in second grade to quickly make everything from men's coats to ball gowns. Just fold a rectangle end to end, side to side. At the folded point, snip out a tiny opening for the neckline. Open out the rectangle and cut a slit from the hem to the opening. Sew the sides together leaving space below the fold for an armhole. If you want long sleeves, make the rectangle wide enough to include them, and sew the underarm sleeve curve when you sew the sides together. If you

Rows of running stitches can be pulled into gathers for a decorative touch at the shoulders or across the chest.

want short sleeves, cut a narrower rectangle. Make "smocking" and sleeveless dresses with rows of running stitches at the shoulders and across the chest. Machine hem the bottom and glue on lace or whatever you choose for trim. Narrow ribbons or scraps of selvedge make fine belts.

*I*f you enjoy making an easy gift that delights a friend, you will enjoy making a drawstring bag. The bag fits neatly inside a larger purse, and whips out easily when someone wants to show a

RIBBON PRINT DRAWSTRING BAG

grandchild's picture. The bag has enough room above the heads of the photoprint figures for the gathers not to interfere with the photo.

The chart on page 83 will save time when you need to make a special but hurry-up gift. Just find your photograph's vertical measurement at the top of the chart. Look down the column to find the size for cutting the pieces. You'll find it all worked out: where to place the plate for printing the ribbon bag, where to mark to insert the photoprint for the folded bag, etc.

Trim the printing plate carefully to avoid unsightly black lines at the edge of the figure. Print it on the ribbon.

You can also use the chart for printing horizontal images. Cut out the pieces using the measurements from the chart. You'll need two outer bag pieces, two lining pieces, and one ribbon that's a little wider than the image you want to print.

To print the ribbon, first cut the mending fabric to a rectangular shape larger than the image you wish to print, and transfer the image plus its surroundings to the plate. Color the figure with markers or water-softened colored pencils. Cut the figure out of the plate. Inspect the cutout on white paper. Cut away black lines at any edge; they give the print a pasted look.

Look at the chart to see where to place the bottom of the plate on the ribbon. Print the figure on the ribbon using the "Small Images on Shiny Fabric" technique, page 18.

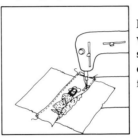

Pad the ribbon with batting and sew it to the center of the front piece.

To soften the print and remove transferability, place the ribbon, face down, on clean typing paper. Iron the wrong side and peel the ribbon from the paper. Repeat ironing on clean sheets of paper until no image comes off.

Place a narrow strip of quilt batting behind the ribbon, then match the center of the printed ribbon to the center of the

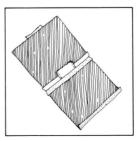

Sew the top edge of each bag piece to a lining piece. Press the seams open; press under 1/4" at the bottom of each lining.

Make a ribbon print
drawstring bag to delight a
friend, and be finished in
an hour. Not only is it
handy to carry things, it's
also fun to show off a
grandchild each time you
pull it out of your purse.
Instructions begin on page
66.

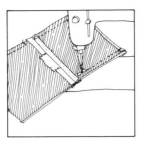

front bag piece and topstitch along the edges of the ribbon.

Using 1/4" seams, sew the lining front to the bag front along the top edge, catching the end of the ribbon in the seam. Do the same with the bag's back and back lining pieces.

Press the seams open. Press the bottom 1/4" of each lining piece to the

Turn the bag right side out and sew the folds of the lining together. Turn the lining inside the bag and press it.

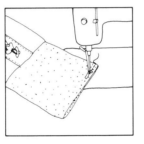

wrong side. Place the front piece on the back piece, right sides facing and with the front lining on top of the back lining. Using 1/4" seams, sew from the folded lower edge of the lining up the side to the seam. Skip 5/8" from the top seam of the bag front, then sew down the side of the front piece, across the lower front, and up the other side in the same way,

again skipping 5/8" of the front piece before the seam.

Turn the bag right side out. Topstitch the two pressed folds of the lining together to close the bag, then fold the lining inside the bag and press. Make a casing at the top of the bag by sewing two rows of stitches all the way around,

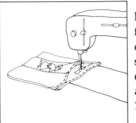

Make a casing for the drawstrings by sewing two rows of stitching, one at 5/8" and one at 1/4" from the top.

one row 5/8" down from the top and the other row 1/4" down from the top.

Thread two drawstrings through the casing, one entering and exiting from the right and the other entering and exiting from the left. Hold the bag open to knot their ends. Tie decorative knots along the tails of the drawstrings.

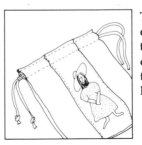

Thread two drawstrings through the casing and hold the bag open to knot their ends.

*T*here are several ways to quilt an image—try one on your drawstring bag.

Trapunto is a traditional method. By hand or machine, sew the printed photo image to a backing fabric

as scissors or a craft knife, a pencil, a large needle, stuffing, and a press cloth.

To block out the figure you wish to quilt, place the photo-printed fabric, right side down, on typing paper on the padded board. Cut a piece of freezer

FOLDED DRAWSTRING BAG WITH TRAPUNTO

by sewing around the outline of the figure close to the printed edge. Leave an opening in a convenient place. Use tweezers to stuff small pieces of stuffing or quilt batting scraps inside the figure. Don't stuff too much, as it distorts the features. Then finish sewing around the figure to close it all up.

Mock trapunto is a quick and easy substitute for the traditional method. Put a piece of quilt batting between the printed fabric and a backing fabric. Sew all around the figure by hand or machine. Then fold the loose edges back and very carefully snip away the batting that surrounds the figure.

No-sew trapunto is a technique I developed for chins and necks. It is useful for photoprints for permanent display in embroidery hoops, boxes, and for other projects that don't need to be washed. And it's for people who, like me, sometimes are just not in the mood to thread a needle. Use this technique for projects that will never be washed.

You will need a fabric photo print, backing fabric (or a cardboard backing if you want to use this technique for a box or framed photo), freezer paper, Pellon Wonder-Under Transfer Webbing® or fusible web with a release sheet, as well

paper larger than the figure. Iron the shiny side of the freezer paper to the wrong side of the fabric print. The shiny side of freezer paper is a thin layer of plastic that will act as a light adhesive when you iron it onto fabric. Tape the print to a window or place it on a light box if you need help to see the outline of the figure, and trace the outline of the figure onto the attached freezer paper. If you wish to give the chin a shape, trace the chin, collar line and two edges of the neck.

Peel back part of the freezer paper and cut on the line to remove the paper from the background.

Peel back part of the freezer paper to cut on the traced line, and remove the paper from the background. You can peel back a bit from the line but keep part of the freezer paper fastened to the printed figure to maintain its placement. You can use a craft knife for cutting the paper if you're careful not to cut the fabric, but scissors are safer. Remove the

69

freezer paper from the sections that you wish to flatten, like the neck and the background. Do not remove the paper from sections that you wish to round, like the face and the body.

Place the print face down on typing paper on the padding. Cut a piece of Wonder-Under® or other fusible web with a release backing to the same size as the piece of fabric and apply it to the wrong side of the print as directed by the manufacturer of the web. This will make the print into an iron-on appliqué. Be sure that the adhesive web is applied to the background all around the figure. The web will cover the freezer paper silhouette. You do not need to remove the freezer paper silhouette.

To fuse the print to the backing and to stuff the figure, position the fabric print, fusible side down, on the backing fabric or cardboard. Place a damp press cloth on the fabric print. Following directions for Wonder-Under® or the fusible web, fuse the head area and the background section above and beside it, up to but not including the neck.

When the fused section is dry and cool, insert the blunt end of a large needle at the neck to open the pocket between the fabric print and the freezer paper. Stuff small pieces of cotton or batting into the pocket to round the face.

Now place a damp press cloth on top of the print. Fuse the neck firmly. Fuse both sides of the torso to the background but leave the bottom open. Use the needle again to separate the fabric torso from the freezer paper. Stuff the torso from the bottom, then use your hot iron to fuse the bottom opening closed.

There's your trapunto figure with no sewing at all.

Print and quilt a fabric photograph by any of these methods, then construct the folded drawstring bag. Refer to the chart on page 83 for the size to cut the outer bag and lining pieces. Fold the outer bag fabric at the middle and press with an iron to mark the bag bottom. Open out the bag and mark the location for the bottom of the opening where the print will be inserted, using the figure from the chart and measuring that distance up from the fold. Use the slash-fold-top-stitch method described on page 50 to make the opening and insert the print.

Fold the bag fabric on the crease, right sides together, and sew each side with a 1/4" seam from the fold to 1½" away from the raw edge at the top of the bag. On this last 1½", press the 1/4" seam allowances to the wrong side and top-stitch them. This will make a neat opening for the drawstrings. Fold the two top flaps to the inside along a line 7/8" from the raw edge.

Fold the lining piece in half and, right sides together, sew the sides with a 1/4" seam. Around the top edge, press 1/4" to the wrong side. Insert the lining into the bag, and topstitch 1/8" down from the folded top to join the lining to the bag while also forming the lower line of the casing.

Now stitch again all around the top of the bag 1/4" from the folded edge of the bag. This forms the top of the casing. Insert two drawstrings, each entering and exiting from its own opening at the opposite sides of the bag. Knot the ends of each.

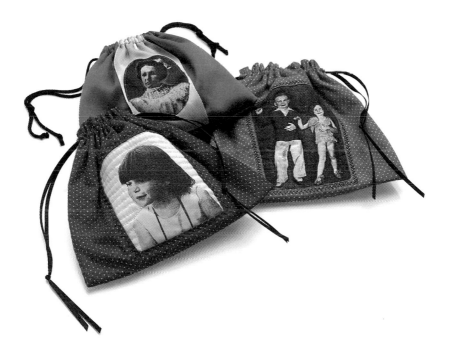

Try one of the methods of
trapunto quilting as you
make this little drawstring
bag. Read how to do it
beginning on page 69.

*H*ere is another project that uses trapunto on a hand-colored fabric print. Or you can outline quilt or background quilt the figures.

Outline quilting creates an indentation

TAP DANCERS PILLOW

beside the figure and an effect similar to trapunto. To prevent distortion, sew a little bit away from the figure's edge. In outline quilting by machine, always begin sewing at the top of the head of the figure at the center of the picture. Sew to outline one half of the figure. Stop at the bottom and cut the thread. Return to the top of the head and sew to outline the other half. Don't sew to shape arms and other body parts until the figure is fully outlined. If you sew chins and necks you may spend as much time as I do ripping them out.

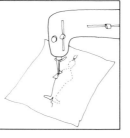

Outline stitch one side of the figure from the center top, then begin at the top again to outline the other side.

Background quilting flattens the background, causing a rounded figure to emerge. Outline quilt the figure first, then begin at the upper corner and sew back and forth across the print. Use the presser foot as a guide for sewing horizontal lines that are somewhat even, running the previous line of stitching along the edge of the presser foot as you

sew the next line. The drawstring bag on page 72 was background quilted in this manner.

For this project, add borders to the quilted fabric photo to make the pillow front match a purchased pillow form. You may be surprised to discover that making an object that must be a particular size is easier than being free to choose any size or design you wish. Limits can be freeing if not carried to extremes; with any option possible, decisions can be hard to make.

Stack the fabric photo, batting, and backing, then quilt the background in horizontal lines.

Print and color your photograph. Then, before you do anything else, quilt your photograph. This is very important. If the photographed figures are large, it's even more important! The larger the figures the more the photograph will shrink when quilted, and it will shrink unevenly, so the edges may be very rippled. So always quilt the photograph before calculating and cutting the bordering frames of the pillow or block. Before quilting, the tap dancers snapshot was 3" by 4½". After quilting, it was only 2⅞" by 4⅜". If I had cut the strips before quilting, I could have adjusted the size by sewing one seam slightly narrower. But a larger image would have shrunk more. I would have needed to do quite a lot of alterations.

Quilt the fabric photo then measure its shortest height and width. Mark, sew, and cut it square.

After you've printed, colored, and quilted the photograph completely, you need to square the photoprint. Measure the shortest distance across the quilted image in both horizontal and vertical directions. These will be the dimensions of the quilt block. Use a carpenter's square or other right angle to mark a perfect rectangle at those dimensions, then machine sew on the marked line and trim outside it. Now, measure the rectangle again. All further decisions will be based on the colors and the size of the quilted print.

For this Tap Dancers Pillow, the border colors had personal meaning to me. Sewing them onto the old snapshot that had been buried in my childhood album brought back happy memories. The bright pink was the costume's color, and the inexpensive fabric was scratchy like the costume; the berry red was the color of my last costume. The pin-dot black seemed an echo of the black-and-white floor tiles and the girl's top hat—almost a sound, like a delicate rhythm of children's tap shoes. Too close to the image, the black would have overpowered it; too far away, it would be lost. I enjoyed making the pillow—that was the purpose of making the pillow, to be happy.

Square the quilted fabric photo, select your border fabrics, and cut them to size. The chart on page 82 will help you decide what size to make the borders. Starting with the inner border color and the strip that goes at the top edge of the fabric photo, place the border piece, right side down, on top of the fabric photo piece and sew a 1/4" seam. Do the same with the bottom border piece. Press these two pieces flat, then sew on the side pieces in the same way. Continue by adding the top and bottom sections of the next border color, pressing them, and then adding the side pieces.

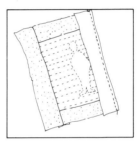

Attach the top and bottom border pieces, press them, then add the side border pieces.

When the pillow top is as big as you want it, cut a piece of fabric for the pillow back, using the same fabric as the outer border of the front but cutting it big enough to allow for a zipper. Insert the zipper, then unzip it about an inch. Sew the front and back pieces together, right sides facing, rounding the corners as you sew. Open the zipper completely and turn the pillow cover right side out. Try it on the pillow form. If it fits snugly, turn the cover wrong side out again and trim the seams and corners. Sign it on the inside, then turn it right side out and put in the pillow form.

73

With trapunto, outline, and
background quilting as
well as several colors of
borders, a small snapshot
becomes a beautiful
memoir.
Instructions for this pillow
begin on page 72.

My friend came for a visit
and made me this pillow in
a day, including the trip to
the fabric store! It's fast,
easy, and dramatic—what
more could you ask?
See page 76 for instructions.

_T_his great pillow was a gift, the first fabric photoprint gift anyone's ever given me. My artist friend Elaine Lackey made it when she came to visit and found fabric prints of my family many patches together, right sides together, to make a length that will cross the foundation at an angle. Then sew another set of patches together the same way. (Don't cut the patches to size. Just sew two large scraps together, look at

EASY-DOES-IT CRAZY-QUILT PILLOW

scattered about my studio. It only took her a day, including a visit to a thrift shop that provided much of the fabric. What a gift! I sure hope she comes back soon!

To make a pillow like this, you'll need fabric photographs in a variety of sizes, an 18" pillow form, velvet and satin fabric scraps (thrift shops and yard sales are good places to find a variety of old fabrics), a 20" by 22" piece of velveteen or other fabric for the back of the pillow, a 20" square of muslin or other sturdy scrap fabric, an 18" zipper for the back of the pillow, muslin for covering the pillow form, heavy-duty yellow thread, batting or fleece, and a sewing machine that can do embroidery stitches.

what you have, and then, if you like it, trim the seam allowance.) Place one strip of patches, right side up, on the 20" foundation fabric. Right sides together, place a second strip of patches on top. Machine sew a straight line to join them to

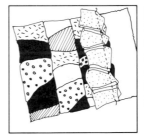

Flip the top strip flat and add another strip in the same way; continue until the foundation fabric is covered.

Make strips of crazy patches, lay one on the foundation and another face to face with it, and sew them to the foundation.

each other and to the foundation. Flip over the top set of patches so it's right side up. If you like it, trim the allowance away from both strips. Continue sewing and flipping strips of patches, perhaps placing individual patches between, until the 20" foundation is covered. The edges can be crooked, since you'll cut them off.

Press the pillow top with a steam iron. Sew machine embroidery stitches at the edges of the patches. (At last! a use for those machine embroidery stitches.)

Make several fabric photos and color them. Fold their edges under. Spend no time at all deciding where they're to go.

To make the crazy-patch pillow top, first sew solid-colored scraps of velvet and satin to the foundation, crazy-quilt fashion. One way to do this is to sew

Just put them on at angles, crossing the patches, or fitting them into some of the patches if it feels right.

Cut pieces of batting to fit under the prints if you wish. Baste the prints in position on the crazy-patch top, slipping the batting in after basting three sides. Machine embroider the edges of the prints to join them to the crazy-patch pillow top.

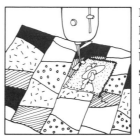

Place the fabric photos in position and baste on three sides, slip in a piece of batting, then machine embroider the edges.

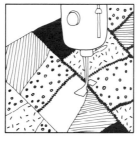

Sew machine embroidery stitches at the edges of the patches, using a contrasting color of thread.

Cut across the velveteen backing fabric about 3" from one short edge. Apply the zipper. Trim the backing and the crazy quilt front each to 19" square.

Right sides together, pin the velveteen back to the crazy-patch front. Use a salad plate or round ice cream carton as a template to draw a curve at each corner. This prevents dog-eared points at the pillow corners. Open the zipper about an inch. Sew the pillow together 1/2" from the raw edge. Open the zipper and turn the pillow right side out.

Sew a muslin covering for the pillow form by sewing around three sides. Turn it right side out and slip the pillow into the covering. Slipstitch the opening closed. Try the pillow inside the crazy-

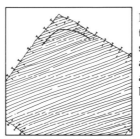

Pin the back to the front, right sides together, and draw curves at each corner before sewing.

patch cover. If it fits well, remove the pillow and trim away the excess fabric from the curves you marked at the corners of the cover. Sign your name inside the cover, insert the pillow form, and zip the zipper.

77

*I*f you can guide two raw edges of fabric along the side of your sewing machine's presser foot, you can make this quilt. There's only a small bit of hand sewing, hidden on the back, and the rest is by

MODIFIED LOG CABIN QUILT

machine. If you enjoy puzzles, you'll enjoy puzzling out the pieces.

My log cabin photo quilt, shown on the back cover of this book, is a modification of a well-known quilting pattern; here the traditional design is used as a border around the fabric photos.

I used nine photos for a three-by-three block square quilt. Use any number you wish, arranging them in a rectangle. The photographs can be as small as a 3-by-4-inch snapshot or as large as 8 by 10 inches; you'll add borders as needed to make all the photoprints into blocks of a single size.

First print, color, and quilt each photograph. Fabric photos shrink when you quilt them; the larger the figures the

Quilt each fabric photo then mark it with a carpenter's square. Machine stitch and trim to the new reduced size.

more the quilting will pull in the edges. They will pull in more at the center where the stuffing is thickest and the edges will be very uneven. One big photograph on my quilt shrank a full inch in

height and width at the middle, none at the corners. Unfortunately, I had sewed on the border strips before quilting, so I had a lot of ripping out to do.

After quilting, trim each fabric photo using a carpenter's square or other right-angle device to draw a rectangle of the narrowest width and shortest height of the quilted cloth. Machine sew along the line and then cut just outside it.

If you're eager to start sewing, you can print, color, and quilt one photograph, trim it, and sew on the strips to make one block of the quilt. Then, with

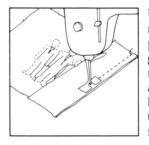

Use your machine's presser foot as a guide to make a narrow seam, attaching the border strip to the quilted fabric photo.

a long machine stitch, sew the quilt block into a pillow. You'll have it to admire while making the other blocks, and you can easily take it apart when you are ready to assemble the quilt top.

Choose your border colors to harmonize with the quilt images. I used four shades each of blue and green so that I could progress from light near the fabric photo to dark at the outer edges of the block. When I assembled the quilt top, I arranged the blue and green blocks checkerboard fashion, then added a strip of burgundy around the edge of the quilt. If your images are of children, using scraps from their clothes would be a lovely touch.

Now, measure one quilted fabric photo rectangle again. On the chart on page 82, fill in the blanks with the vertical and horizontal measurements of this photoprint. In my quilt, the blocks are 15 inches finished; use that figure or one of your own. Determine the total widths of the borders by filling in the blanks, then divide that to use two or more border fabrics. I used four borders on each fabric photo, varying their width for smaller or larger photos. But I suggest you make things easier for yourself: use fewer strips around the large pictures, more around the little ones. The quilt will be more exciting if you vary the width of the borders. Add 1/2 inch seam allowances and cut long strips to those widths.

Pin a strip of vertical border A to one side of the photoprint. Right sides facing, match the strip's long raw edge with the edge of the trimmed fabric photo, aligning the end of the border strip with the upper edge of the fabric photo. Use your sewing machine's presser foot as a guide to make a narrow seam—just

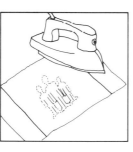

Press the border strips outward, being careful not to touch the fabric photo with the hot iron.

guide the raw edge along the side of the presser foot. Cut the long tail of the border strip even with the lower edge of the photoprint. Pin and sew the strip to the opposite side, then trim it even.

Press these two border strips outward, being sure not to touch the photoprint with the hot iron. Pressing the fabric photo will flatten the batting, so be careful to press only the seam and the border.

Pin and sew the horizontal strip of border A to the upper edge of the block, across both side borders as well as the photoprint. Do the same with the lower border, and press them outward. That completes the first border color (border A) on the first fabric photo.

Cut the strips for border B. Pin and sew the vertical strips to the sides, press, then add the horizontal strips on the top

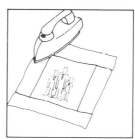

The border strips at the top and bottom of the block are sewn across the photoprint and both side borders.

and bottom. This completes the second border color. Add more border strips in the same way.

Use the chart again to plan the borders for your second photo print. The size of the image will be different, but the

Assemble the quilt top by stitching the blocks into rows and then sewing the rows together.

desired finished size will be the same as that of the first block. All of the blocks should end up the same size—15½ inches square if you are following my example. Continue adding borders to each fabric photo until all of your blocks are completed.

To assemble these blocks into the quilt top, arrange them into a rectangle. Sew them together in horizontal rows; sew the first two blocks of the upper row together, right sides facing, along one edge and then the third block to the second. Make another row of blocks, then sew the two rows of blocks together.

If you want an outer border like the burgundy one in my quilt, add it as you did the other borders, first sewing the sides then pressing before you add the top and bottom borders.

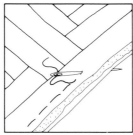

Layer the completed quilt top with batting and a backing fabric and hand baste them together.

Layer the completed quilt top with batting and a backing fabric. Hand baste the layers together, then quilt them by machine sewing in the valley between border strips. Then bind the edges with a strip of border fabric; sew a strip to the outer edge of the quilt top exactly as you did for the other borders, then turn it to the back and hand hem it to its own stitching line.

Or, instead of machine quilting, try Aunt Gwen's finish-your-quilt-in-an-hour technique. (Speedy Aunt Gwen

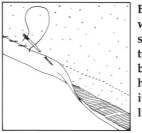

Bind the edges with a border strip that is turned to the back and hand hemmed along its own stitching line.

whips out a dress without a pattern in an hour or two). Lay the whole quilt top, right sides together, on a backing fabric the same size. Sew around three sides, as if you were making a pillowcase. Insert a full-size piece of quilt batting inside. Now, thread a needle with a very long length of heavy thread. Make big stitches across the top of the quilt and little stitches on the bottom to join the top, batting and backing. Cut the thread between the stitches and tie knots. You can tie heavier, decorative thread to those knots. When you've finished, slipstitch the opening closed.

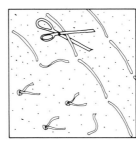

To make a tied quilt, make a line of small stitches far apart on the top of the quilt. Cut the long stitches and tie.

se your imagination to decide what to print and where to print it. Express yourself. An author I know wears a photo of editor Maxwell Perkins, printed on a pocket that holds pencils,

Squeeze dyes, sparkle paints, or puff paints directly from the bottle to color areas between fabric photos.

YOUR OWN PROJECT

when too many words pile up. A biologist friend printed photocopied engravings of the plants that he uses for research. A neighbor printed snapshots of her beloved cat.

Have your child color on erasable bond paper, then use the dry method to transfer the drawing to cloth.

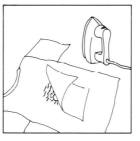

If you give your child erasable bond paper to color with crayons, you can then easily transfer the child's pictures to fabric. You can hand write your poem in pencil and transfer it to your T-shirt.

Print on your blouse, your shorts, your skirt. Decorate your scarf or beach bag. Make a bolo tie. Transfer a child's drawing to his father's necktie, brother's shaving kit, or sister's favorite dress. Considering how imaginative children are, maybe you'd better not tell your child how to make the transfer until the child is old enough to handle an iron. If

your imagination ever needs freshening, talk things over with any four-year-old.

Remember that fabric dyes and paints can be used with fabric photos. You can tie-dye your shirt and then add photoprints. Or you can print your fabric photo and then scribble, drip, and draw with puff paints, sparkles, or dyes that come in small squeeze bottles.

Try other needlework techniques with your fabric photos. Add beads, or embroider to accent details.

Combine fabric photos with embroidery, beadwork, or appliqué.

Self expression is simply a matter of using images that appeal to you, that you feel strongly about, that amuse you, or that are common in your life. As I said in the Introduction, the real fabric of this craft is the fabric of your life.

81

CALCULATING BORDERS FOR A BLOCK

Fill in the blanks of this chart to determine the amount of fabric you need to fill the space between a centered image and an outer sewn edge of a project.

	My Project Vertically **(from top to bottom)**	**My Project Horizontally** **(from side to side)**
Desired finished size	_____ "	_____ "
My image measures	– _____ " vertically	– _____ " horizontally
So I need to fill	= _____ "	_____ "
Divided by	÷ 2	÷ 2
Each half to fill	= _____ " above/below	= _____ " each side

This is the total width of each border. If you wish to make the border of several strips of different colors, you will need to break down these measurements into the widths for narrower borders. Label your borders A, B, and C, etc., then figure like this:

Outline photo with border	– _____ "	Fabric A	– _____ " Fabric A
And a second border	– _____ "	Fabric B	– _____ " Fabric B
The remaining space	= _____ "	Fabric C	– _____ " Fabric C

Check for errors:

Do $(A + B + C) \times 2$ + Vertical image = Desired finished size?

Do $(A + B + C) \times 2$ + Horizontal image = Desired finished size?

Add seam allowances ($2 \times 1/4" = 1/2"$) to each strip. Add seam allowances and cut the strips:

A _____ + 1/2" = _____ " vertical   A _____ + 1/2" = _____ " horizontal

B _____ + 1/2" = _____ " vertical   B _____ + 1/2" = _____ " horizontal

C _____ + 1/2" = _____ " vertical   C _____ + 1/2" = _____ " horizontal

CHART FOR DRAWSTRING BAGS

1. If your photograph's vertical measurement is

2"	2½"	3"	3½"	4"	4½"	5"	5½"	6"

2. The finished size of your bag will be 6½" by

5½"	5½"	5½"	5½"	6"	6¼"	6½"	6¾"	6¾"

TO MAKE THE RIBBON-PRINT BAG

1. Cut the ribbon

6"	6"	6"	6"	6½"	6¾"	7"	7¼"	7¼"

2. Cut two bag pieces and two lining pieces each 7" by

6"	6"	6"	6"	6½"	6¾"	7"	7¼"	7¼"

3. Print the ribbon

4. Place the bottom of your plate this distance from the bottom raw edge of the ribbon

1"	¾"	¾"	¾"	¾"	½"	½"	½"	¼"

TO MAKE THE FOLDED BAG

1. Cut one outer bag piece 7" by

12¾"	12¾"	12¾"	12¾"	13¾"	14¼"	14¾"	15¼"	15¼"

2. Cut one lining piece 7" by

11¾"	11¾"	11¾"	11¾"	12¾"	13¼"	13¾"	14¼"	14¼"

3. Measure up from the fold at the bottom of the bag and mark where to insert your fabric photoprint

¾"	½"	½"	½"	½"	½"	¼"	¼"	0"

Once again I have my toe on my knee.

*I*f you follow the directions in this book carefully, you shouldn't have any trouble at all—this is really a very simple process. But mistakes do seem to creep in.

Often a "mistake" is the first step of a new discovery, so be alert to the possibilities. An odd misprint can look exciting and lead you into a more expressive way of printing your photos. Or the "mistake" can lead you to discover a new bit of technique; much of my own discovery process could have been described as happy accidents.

You may run into occasional problems, but generally they are easy to fix. Here is a list of possible troubles and what to do about each of them.

HOW TO FIX AN IMPERFECT PLATE

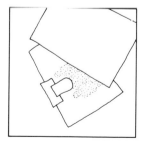

Make a small plate of the section that didn't transfer; cover the rest of the image with paper.

If your plate isn't perfect, you can do what Andy Warhol did and use it anyway. His misprints weren't planned, he just didn't want to take time to register them properly, and he recognized that the mistake produced exciting work.

But if your mother's going to be unhappy at being paler than her sister in the group portrait, you'd better fix the problem on the mending fabric plate before making the final transfer to fabric. Cut another mending fabric patch a little

TROUBLES AND FIXES

larger than the missing section. Cover the successfully transferred section of the photocopy with typing paper to protect your iron's soleplate. Attach a paper handle to the new patch. Heat the patch on the missing section of the photocopy and peel off the new plate. You will now have two plates, a bigger one with a missing part plus a smaller one with that part only.

For the transfer to fabric, you can choose to transfer the larger plate to fabric, then transfer the smaller second plate to the fabric print; or cut the two plates apart and fit them

Cut the two plates and fit them together before transferring to fabric.

together jigsaw-puzzle fashion before transferring to fabric. Butt the edges rather than overlapping them, and use a soft pencil to fill any missing spots on the fabric photo. Make small dots with your pencil rather than hard lines, adding dots until it is dark enough.

HOW TO DEAL WITH WHITE STREAKS ON THE PRINTING PLATE

Streaks on the mending fabric indicate uneven adhesive. Iron the mending fabric onto clean typing paper before making the transfer from paper. Use a soft pencil to correct any unevenness on the fabric photo.

HOW TO MAKE A DARKER PRINT

A moist printing plate will transfer a darker image to fabric than will a dry one. To darken the image on the final transfer, use a steam iron, or cover the plate with a damp press cloth to make the transfer. If you know there is not much ink on your plate, such as a plate that has already been skimmed, wet the plate just before you release print the image to fabric.

To darken a print, you can cover the plate with a damp press cloth before transferring it to cloth.

HOW TO SEPARATE A STUCK PRINTING PLATE FROM FABRIC

Though the printing plate seldom sticks to the fabric, there are several methods to try if it does: place the pieces on a hard surface and iron them with pressure, then pull them apart while they are very hot; iron from the fabric side; or dampen the plate with water or steam, iron it, and pull the pieces apart while they are very hot.

HOW TO STRAIGHTEN A STRETCHED PLATE

It is important to place your paper handle along the grainline on one edge of your mending patch and to pull it with the grain as you remove it from the photocopy. This will usually keep the plate's edges squared. If you pull diagonally by mistake, the image will be distorted. If the image is large and peeled hot, the printing plate's edge can curve.

If a plate's edges are uneven after

Lay the stretched plate face up on heated padding and pull as needed to straighten it.

peeling, heat and stretching will straighten them. The best time to do this is while the plate is still hot from peeling. If it cools, heat the padding with the iron and place the plate, transfer side up, on the hot padding. Place your index finger and thumb at the two corners that have pulled in. Pull the middle of the plate at the opposite end. To straighten more, pull the plate on the bias. Be careful not to transfer hot black ink from your fingertips to white areas of the plate.

HOW TO REMOVE EXTRA ADHESIVE FROM THE FABRIC PHOTO

Scrub the extra adhesive with rubbing alcohol, being careful not to touch the image. If your fabric is not made of acetate, you can rub the adhesive with nail polish remover (acetone). If you're not sure of the fiber content, test a scrap before applying nail polish remover; it dissolves acetate.

HOW TO MAKE A WIDER BORDER AROUND YOUR PHOTOCOPY IMAGE

If the paper image is crowded by others so there's no margin, or if the image you want to print is centered on a black photocopied mat that you don't wish to print, make a white margin by ironing a piece of typing paper onto the black photocopy ink along that side. Because photocopy ink is thermoplastic, it will melt and act as a light adhesive.

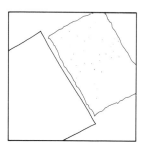

To align a shifty fabric, lay typing paper beside it, line up the edges, then remove the paper.

HOW TO STRAIGHTEN AND CONTROL SHIFTY FABRICS

To straighten silk charmeuse or other shifty fabrics, align one edge with the edge of a piece of typing paper.

HOW TO REMOVE TRANSFERABILITY

If your fabric photo project will be subjected to any rubbing or pressure (as will a bookmark, for example), you'll want to be sure it won't accidentally transfer part of its image onto something else. To remove transferability from a release print, turn it face down on clean typing paper and iron it from the back, repeating with clean paper till no more image transfers to the paper.

HOW TO SOFTEN A RELEASE PRINT

Ironing as you would to remove transferability will also soften the cloth in the print area. To soften it further, stretch the print on the bias to break the bond of the adhesive.

Stretching a print on the bias will soften it because it breaks the bond of the adhesive.

HOW TO FLATTEN THE IMAGE IF YOU OVERSTUFFED IT

If you stuff a figure too much, cover the print with scrap fabric and press lightly with a warm iron. Batting flattens when ironed.

HOW TO REGISTER AN IMAGE

I can't think why you would ever need to register an image, but it's easy to do. Photocopy the image to the center of a blank page. Cut out a mending fabric patch to include wide margins along all four sides of the photocopied image. With a heated iron, fasten one margin of the patch to the white paper area around the image.

Use a ruler to make lines that cross the patch and extend onto the paper. These are registration marks.

Fasten a paper handle to the free edge of the patch. Transfer the image to make the patch into a printing plate, peel it by a dry method, and set it aside. Lower the iron's temperature to minimum heat setting.

Cut out the image from the photocopy to make a window opening in the photocopy,

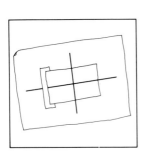

Cut the image from the photocopy to make a small window. Line up the pencil marks and attach the plate to the paper window.

making the hole smaller than the printing plate. This opening will be a stencil. Match the pencil lines of the transferred plate with the lines on the photocopy. Stretch the plate on the bias if needed to make the lines meet. Fasten the plate's four margins to the photocopy window frame with your heated iron.

Cut your cloth to allow a comfortably wide margin. Place the paper mask in the center of the cloth, and transfer the image by the skimming method (page 25). Use the tip of the iron as if it were a pencil to gently stroke the black

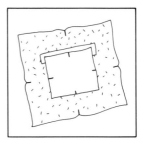

Fold and mark the plate with pencil; fold and mark the fabric with the iron; line up the marks to center the image.

areas; don't stroke the white areas! Peel the plate, using the paper window as a handle.

If your print doesn't need to be perfectly centered, you can position the plate by this easy technique. Fold the fabric you wish to print and use the heated iron to crease four short centering marks at the middle of each edge. Fold the plate gently and use a pencil to mark the dull side along the fold. To position the pieces for printing, use a ruler to line up the pencil marks on the plate with the creases on the fabric.

AFTERWORD

There is a vitality, a life-force, an energy, a quickening that is translated through you into action and because there is only one of you in all of time, this expression is unique. And if you block it, it will never exist through any other medium and be lost. The world will not have it. It is not your business to determine how good it is nor how valuable nor how it compares with other expressions. It is your business to keep it yours clearly and directly, to keep the channel open. You do not even have to believe in yourself or your work. You have to keep open and aware directly to the urges that motivate you. Keep the channel open.

Martha Graham as quoted in *Dance to the Piper* by Agnes De Mille

89

Afterword

BIBLIOGRAPHY

Other Fabric Photoprinting Processes

Gassan, Arnold. *Handbook for Contemporary Photography*. Rochester, New York: Light Impressions, 1977.

House, Suda. *Artistic Photographic Processes*. New York: Watson-Guptill, 1981.

Howell-Koehler, Nancy. *Photo Art Processes*. Worcester, Massachusetts: Davis, 1980.

Nettles, Bea. *Breaking the Rules: A Photo Media Cookbook*. Rochester, New York: Light Impressions, 1977.

Newman, Thelma R. *Innovative Printmaking*. New York: Crown, 1977.

Sacilotto, Deli. *Photographic Printmaking Techniques*. New York: Watson-Guptill, 1982.

Wade, Kent E. *Alternative Photographic Processes*. Dobbs Ferry, New York: Morgan and Morgan, 1978.

Silkscreen Printing

Biegeleisen, J. I. *Screen Printing: A Contemporary Guide*. New York: Watson-Guptill, 1971.

Eichenberg, Fritz. *Lithography and Silkscreen*. New York: Abrams, 1978.

Fossett, R. O. *Screen Printing Photographic Techniques*. Cincinnati, Ohio: Signs of the Times, 1973.

Hindley, Geoffrey. *Working with Light-Sensitive Materials*. New York: Van Nostrand Reinhold, 1978.

Inko. *Silk Screen Printing: Materials and Techniques*. Catalog. Oakland, California: Screen Process Supplies Manufacturing Company, 1971.

Saff, Donald, and Deli Sacilotto. *Screenprinting: History and Process*. New York: Holt, Rinehart and Winston, 1979.

Schwalbach, Mathilda V. and James A. *Silk-Screen Printing for Artists and Craftsmen*. New York: Dover, 1980.

Valentino, Richard, and Phyllis Mufson. *Fabric Printing: Screen Method*. San Francisco: Bay Books, 1975.

Design

Albers, Josef. *Interaction of Color*. Westford, Massachusetts: Yale University Press, 1963.

Allen, Virginia P., and Dot Guilding. Pre-Quilted Crafts. East Lansing, Michigan: Spinning Spool, 1976.

Birren, Faber. *The Textile Colorist*. New York: Van Nostrand Reinhold, 1980.

Bothwell, Dorr, and Marlys Frey. *Notan: The Dark-Light Principle of Design*. New York: Van Nostrand Reinhold, 1968.

Edwards, Betty. *Drawing on the Artist Within*. New York: Simon and Schuster, 1986.

Edwards, Betty. *Drawing on the Right Side of the Brain*. New York: St. Martin's Press, 1979.

Gray, Bill. *More Studio Tips for Artists and Graphic Designers*. New York: Van Nostrand Reinhold, 1978.

Gray, Bill. *Studio Tips for Artists and Graphic Designers*. New York: Van Nostrand Reinhold, 1976.

Itten, Johannes. *The Elements of Color*. New York: Van Nostrand Reinhold, 1970.

Johnson, Pauline. *Creating with Paper*. Seattle: University of Washington Press, 1958.

Svennas, Elsie. *Advanced Quilting*. New York: Scribners, 1980.

Quilting

Avery, Virginia. *The Big Book of Appliqué*. New York: Scribners, 1978.

Bonesteel, Georgia. *Lap Quilting with Georgia Bonesteel*. Birmingham, Alabama: Oxmoor House, 1982.

Campbell-Harding, Valerie, and Michel Walker. *Every Kind of Patchwork*. Tunbridge Wells, Kent TN2 3DR, England: Search Press, 1983.

Doriss, Barbara Bell. *The Original Log Cabin Jacket and Vest Book*. Atlanta: Yours Truly, 1983.

Fanning, Robbie and Tony. *The Complete Book of Machine Quilting*. Radnor, Pennsylvania: Chilton, 1980.

Haywood, Dixie. *Crazy Quilt Patchwork*. Mineola, New York: Dover, 1986.

Hopkins, Mary Ellen. *The It's Okay if You Sit on my Quilt Book*. Atlanta: Yours Truly, 1982.

James, Michael. *The Second Quiltmaker's Handbook*. Englewood Cliffs, New Jersey: Prentice Hall, 1981.

Laury, Jean Ray. *Quilts and Coverlets*. New York: Van Nostrand Reinhold, 1970.

Malone, Maggie. *Quilting Shortcuts*. New York: Sterling, 1986.

Newman, Thelma R. *Quilting, Patchwork, Appliqué, and Trapunto*. New York: Crown, 1974.

Raymo, Anne, and Holly Vose. *Sew-Up Art*. New York: Music Sales Corporation, 1976.

Wilson, Erica. *Erica Wilson's Quilts of America*. Birmingham, Alabama: Oxmoor House, 1979.

Dollmaking

Fling, Helen. *Marionettes: How to Make and Work Them*. New York: Dover, 1973.

Fraser, Peter. *Introducing Puppetry*. New York: Watson-Guptill, 1968.

Guild, Vera P. *Dollmaker's Workshop*. New York: Hearst, 1981.

Laury, Jean Ray. *Doll Making*. New York: Van Nostrand Reinhold, 1970.

Worrell, Estelle Ansley. *The Doll Book*. New York: Van Nostrand Reinhold, 1966.

Dyeing

Blumenthal, Betsy, and Kathryn Kreider. *Hands on Dyeing*. Loveland, Colorado: Interweave Press, 1988.

Johnson, Meda Parker, and Glen Kaufman. *Design on Fabric*. Second Edition. New York: Van Nostrand Reinhold, 1981.

Resources—Iron-On Mending Fabrics

Packages of iron-on mending fabrics are displayed in the sewing notions departments of fabric, grocery, and variety stores. Look for these brands:

Coats & Clark Iron-On Mending Fabric, Coats & Clark, 30 Patewood Drive, Greenville, SC 29615.

Singer Mending Fabric, Singer Sewing Co., Edison, NH 08837.

Dritz Iron-On Mending Fabric, Dritz Corporation, Spartanburg, SC 29304.

EZ Irontex No-Sew Mending Fabric, 130 Grand St., Carlstadt, NJ 07072.

Wrights Bondex Iron-On Fabric Mending Tape, Wm. E. Wright, West Warren, MA 01092.

Sewing Bee, Talon American, Stamford, CT 06905.

INDEX

afterword 89
background quilting 72, 74
bibliography 90–91
block an image 42
blueprinting 4, 6
book cover project 47, 49
bookmark project 19–22
border prints from snapshots 37–39
borders 73, 82
brownprinting 4
coarse texture fabrics 17, 19–22, 46
color printing 29–31
color copiers 4, 29
color test 30–31
copiers 13, 14
crazy quilt pillow project 75–77
darker print 86
De Mille, Agnes 89
delicate fabrics 26–27
different background 37
direct ironing to cloth 36
doll project 63–65
Double Wedding Ring design 8
dry method 14–16, 23, 34
dye 29–30, 81
embossed image 43
extra adhesive on fabric photo 87
fabric selection 14, 17, 18
facial expression change 43
final transfer, 17–18, 20, 23
    printing plate to fabric
first transfer, 16, 18, 20, 23
    paper to printing plate
flatten overstuffed image 87–88
folded drawstring bag project 69–71, 83
freezer paper 39, 63–64
graduation flap bag project 61–62
Graduation Quilt 8–11, 35
Graham, Martha 89
grandparents pillow project 50, 52
gum printing 4
imperfect plate 85
Inkodyeing 4
Kwik-Printing 4
Lackey, Elaine 50, 51, 76
large images 19–22, 40–42, 61–62
medallion jewelry box project 54–57
mending fabric 3, 7, 13, 15
mirror image 44
mistakes 85
mock trapunto 69
modified log cabin 78–80, back cover
    quilt project
montage 43

natural fibers 17, 20
newsprint ink transfer 33–34
no-sew trapunto 69–70
odd shape image 19
odd-shaped image 34
other fabric printing techniques 4
outline quilting 72, 74
oval image 34, 54
padding 14
paper handle 15, 16, 17, 20, 34
peeling 17, 20
photo-linening 4
photocopy quality 13
placement of a row of images 39
potholder project 51, 53
printed text transfer 33–34
printing process summary 12, 20
projects 45–84
quilting 46, 50, 51, 61, 69–70, 72, 74, 78, 80
register an image 34, 88
release printing 17–22, 25, 29, 30, 33, 35, 39, 42,
    64, 86
remove transferability 87
reverse an image 35–36
ribbon print drawstring bag project 66–68, 83
shifty fabrics 87
shiny fabrics 18, 66
silkscreen printing 4
skimming 25–28, 33, 50, 58, 86, 88
slash-fold-topstitch 50, 59, 70
small images 18, 66
soft photo project 46, 48
soften the print 66, 87
square the photoprint 73, 78
storage of printing plates 17
straighten plate 86
stretched plate 86
strip printing 19–22, 24
stuck plate on fabric 86
synthetic fabrics 17, 18
tap dancers pillow project 51, 72–74
test 14–16
test strip 13
transfer paper 4, 6
trapunto 69–70, 74
troubles and fixes 85–88
velvet printing 58
washing fabric photos 30
wedding invitation box project 58–60
wet rubbing 23–24, 34, 45
white streaks on the printing plate 86
wider border around photocopy image 87
your own project 81